digital character animation 2, volume I: essential techniques

george maestri

New Riders

201 West 103rd Street, Indianapolis, Indiana, 46290

Executive Editor
Steve Weiss

Acquisitions Editor
Laura Frey

Development Editor
Audrey Doyle

Technical Editor
Angie Jones

Managing Editor
Sarah Kearns

Copy Editor
Nancy Albright

Indexer
Cheryl Landis
Craig Small

**Software Development
Specialist**
Jason Haines

Proofreader
Linda Seifert

Production
Jennifer Eberhard
Wil Cruz

Digital Character Animation 2, Volume I: Essential Techniques

By George Maestri

Published by:
New Riders Publishing
201 West 103rd Street
Indianapolis, IN 46290 USA

International Standard Book Number: 1-56205-930-0

Library of Congress Catalog Card Number: 99-63129

Printed in the United States of America

This book was produced digitally by Macmillan Computer Publishing and manufactured using computer-to-plate technology (a film-less process) by GAC, Indianapolis, Indiana.

First Printing: August, 1999

03 02 01 00 99   7 6 5 4 3 2 1

Interpretation of the printing code: The rightmost double-digit number is the year of the book's printing; the rightmost single-digit number is the number of the book's printing. For example, the printing code 99-1 shows that the first printing of the book occurred in 1999.

93-41864

About the Author

George Maestri has worked as a writer, director, and producer in both traditional and computer animation for such companies as Nickelodeon, Warner Brothers, Disney, Comedy Central, Film Roman, MGM, ABC, CBS, and Fox, among others. He was the original animation producer on the Comedy Central series, "South Park" and was nominated for a Cable Ace award for writing on the Nickelodeon series, "Rocko's Modern Life." He has written several books including *[digital] Character Animation* for New Riders Publishing, and numerous articles on computer animation for magazines such as Digital Magic, Computer Graphics World, DV, and New Media, among others.

Dedication

This book is dedicated to Moyet and Preston.

Acknowledgments

Many thanks to Angie Jones for being a wonderful technical editor as well as my conscience. Also thanks to her for many of the animations on the CD, as well as for modeling most of the facial animation targets used in Chapter 10.

Thanks to Tuong Nguyen for the great sculptures used in Chapter 1.

Thanks to the people on the CG-CHAR list for all the great advice.

Thanks to Audrey Doyle for being a terrific editor.

Thanks to Laura Frey, Steve Weiss, Alicia Buckley, David Dwyer, and everyone else at New Riders for letting me create this book as I envisioned it.

Publisher's Note

New Riders would like to congratulate author George Maestri for creating this [digital] masterpiece.

A special debt is owed to Jennifer Eberhardt, Sarah Kearns, Linda Seifert, and Wil Cruz for sharing their amazing talents for this project.

Trademark Acknowledgments

All terms mentioned in this book that are known to be trademarks or service marks have been appropriately capitalized. New Riders Publishing cannot attest to the accuracy of this information. Use of a term in this book should not be regarded as affecting the validity of any trademark or service mark.

Warning and Disclaimer

Every effort has been made to make this book as complete and as accurate as possible, but no warranty or fitness is implied. The information provided is on an "as is" basis. The authors and the publisher shall have neither liability nor responsibility to any person or entity with respect to any loss or damages arising from the information contained in this book or from the use of the CD or programs accompanying it.

Tell Us What You Think!

As the reader of this book, you are our most important critic and commentator. We value your opinion and want to know what we're doing right, what we could do better, what areas you'd like to see us publish in, and any other words of wisdom you're willing to pass our way.

As the Executive Editor for the Professional Graphics team at New Riders Publishing, I welcome your comments. You can fax, email, or write me directly to let me know what you did or didn't like about this book—as well as what we can do to make our books stronger.

Please note that I cannot help you with technical problems related to the topic of this book, and that due to the high volume of mail I receive, I might not be able to reply to every message.

When you write, please be sure to include this book's title and author, as well as your name and phone or fax number. I will carefully review your comments and share them with the author and editors who worked on the book.

Fax: 317-581-4663
Email: newriders@mcp.com

Mail: Steve Weiss
         Executive Editor
         Professional Graphics
         New Riders Publishing
         201 West 103rd Street
         Indianapolis, IN 46290 USA

Contents at a Glance

Table of Contents

Introduction

Animating with a computer is very similar to writing with a word processor. Both are creative tasks that just happen to involve technology. In both cases, creativity, not technology, is what matters. People—not computers—are creative. Technology is simply a tool that helps things along.

A word processor may make your documents look stunningly beautiful, with dozens of fonts in full color, but it does not make you a better writer. Writing is a creative task that comes mostly from the right side of a person's brain. The word processor doesn't read the classics, it doesn't study poetry, and it can't create a brilliant novel, script, or research paper—it takes a creative person to do that. The word processor simply makes it easier to get the words out of your head and onto a printed page so people can read them.

The same goes for computer animation. You may have the best animation software in the world, and it may render each frame of your animation beautifully and quickly, but the content of those frames is limited by your knowledge and creativity. Character animation is a study of motion, timing, and acting, and is just as creative an art as writing, acting, drawing, or painting. Like the word processor, the computer is simply a tool that makes it easier to get the animation out of your head and onto film or videotape so that people can see it.

Just because you animate with a CPU doesn't mean you're some kind of trailblazer in the world of animation. Digital animation may be relatively new, but people have been animating since motion pictures were invented. The skills and knowledge that animators discovered long ago are the foundation upon which computer animators now stand. The computer does make the creation of animation easier and quicker, but it also makes it easier and quicker to make garbage. In order to produce quality animation, you need a firm grounding in the basics of animation, which have not changed since the golden age of animation over 50 years ago. The same principles and techniques that went into the classic cartoons of the 1940's are principles and techniques every animator should know today, regardless of the medium.

Animation is the art, computers are the medium. Whether you animate with pencils, clay, or pixels, you need to know the basics of animation.

You need to understand anatomy, motion, weight, and timing—the foundations of animation. Some animators may draw, some may sculpt, but all stand on the same foundation.

What You Can Expect from This Book

For this second edition, the book has been broken up into two volumes. This volume is meant to give you the basics of designing, building, and animating characters. The second volume goes deeper into the technical issues of animation and character building, as well as the art of making films.

What You Should Know

Before you begin this book, you should have a fundamental understanding of computers, computer graphics, and 3D software. This book will not bore you with a dissertation on CPUs, RAM, and hard disks; nor will it bother you by explaining such things as pixels, alpha channels, and rendering. If you don't know these terms, then you need to study the fundamentals of computer graphics. You should also be familiar with your chosen 3D software. Work through your software's manuals and tutorials to understand its features.

What You Will Need

All you need to animate characters digitally is a computer and a 3D package. An extremely basic package will only handle simple characters, however, and some packages lend themselves to character animation more readily than others. Look for packages that support features such as shape animation, skeletal deformation, multiple target morphing, and inverse kinematics, among others.

Beginning animators should decide on the software they want to use before buying any hardware. Each hardware platform has its selling points, but it's the software that will animate your characters. When buying hardware, always try to buy the fastest machine with the most memory. Systems become obsolete so quickly, so an investment in a fast machine will last much longer than an investment in a slower one. Of course, if you're broke, it is still entirely possible to produce terrific animation on almost any budget, and used equipment can be the basement animator's secret weapon. Quality is not a function of processor speed.

The real lure of digital animation is interactivity, or the ability to play back your animations on the fly and make changes immediately. The faster your machine, the higher the level of interactivity and the smoother the flow of the creative process. To help speed things along, a 3D accelerator card helps you play back shaded animation tests interactively as you create. Not all 3D cards are created equal, so check with your software vendor for a list of supported 3D cards before you buy.

Another important issue is output. Almost any computer can play back thumbnail-sized animations directly on your computer screen. For your own tests, this type of playback is perfectly acceptable. If you want to print to videotape, however, you will need to include a full motion video card for final output. These cards come in many flavors—some only output analog video, some only digital video, some both. This choice will depend on your choice for final output. If you own only a VHS deck, then analog will have to do. Once printed to tape, anybody can view your creations.

About This Book's Approach to Software

It would have been much easier to write this book using specific software packages. A tutorial using Brand X software would prove to be somewhat useless to the person using Brand Y software. Added to that is the fact that as soon as Brand X got a slew of new features or a new interface, this book would be headed for the trash. Besides, there's already a book about the software you own; it's called the manual.

This book takes on a bigger challenge—a guide to anyone with a computer and a 3D package. The principles presented here are done from a package-neutral standpoint. Hopefully, this book will be applicable over a broad range of platforms. To this effect, the book focuses on the many features of these packages that are similar.

The more you work with different 3D packages, the more you will realize how similar they really are to each other. Polygonal modeling in one package is very similar to polygonal modeling in another. Some of the terminology may be a bit different between packages, but the underlying geometry and placement of detail on the model is identical.

This book does have to jump through a few hoops when it comes to terminology. The exact same feature on one package may be called something completely different on another package. When a conflict existed, we tried to choose the term most commonly used among all packages.

A Final Note

Animating characters is a life-long journey, and this book will help you take only the first few steps. Animation can be incredibly fun, but it's also a very difficult art to master. After finishing this book, it will take many years of practice to become a true animator. Hopefully, you will rely on this reference throughout your journey.

CHAPTER 1

Basics of Design

This book is about creating and bringing characters to life. Before you model and animate a character, however, you need to think about its design. A character design can be as simple as a sketch, or as complex as fully rendered sculpture. The design serves as a simple road map, a plan of action for creating a character digitally.

Design means making decisions about your characters. You need to decide how tall or short they'll be, the textures you'll use for their skin, and what type of clothes they'll wear. You also need to decide just how realistic or stylized you want to make your characters. A realistic-looking character means it should be animated realistically as well.

Designing your characters properly makes their personalities jump off the screen. Your audience will know who your characters are immediately—and like them. A well-designed character is also a character that will be easy for you to animate. If you can animate your character without fuss, it makes the animation process easier and far more creative. Designing characters that animate well requires a knowledge of anatomy as well as a good understanding of the strengths and weaknesses of your software tools.

Approaching Design as an Artist

Just like animation, design is an art. When great design is coupled with great animation, the results are much larger than the whole. There are many ways to approach the design of your characters. Design is a creative process, so everyone approaches the task using his or her own artistic strengths and weaknesses. Some people work out their designs with pencil and paper, others prefer clay, some prefer pixels. All these methods can inspire new and innovative designs.

Knowing Your Character

When designing a character, you first need to know a bit about him or her. Is the character young or old, short or tall? Is the character the hero or the villain? Is the character the star of the film or only a bit player? Aggressive or meek? All these criteria, plus many more, will factor into the designs of your characters.

Many times, the script provides clues to the character, and perhaps even a written description. If you are designing a character for your own project, you may want to write down some of the major character traits before you begin the design. A short biography of the character might help as well.

Making Design Decisions

Those who want realistic characters may simply place a human in a laser scanner and snap a digital picture of the real thing. Deciding who steps into the scanner, however, is a design decision. It's important that you consider your character from a design standpoint before you ever touch hand to mouse.

First and foremost, a well-designed character conveys personality. Your characters should also be well-proportioned and appealing to the eye. Even the villain needs to be appealing—particularly if it is in a delightfully gruesome way. In addition to your character's outward appearance, you also need to design with animation in mind. This means understanding your software and what it needs to animate a character successfully.

Some of your design decisions will be dictated by the limitations of your software. If your software doesn't allow you to create hair, for instance, you might want to avoid animating an Old English sheepdog.

You should use the strong points of your software to your advantage and design around the weak spots. No one will know that you didn't have that whizbang new hair plug-in. Instead, the audience simply sees a character on the screen. If it looks good, and has character, it doesn't matter how you created it, even if it's bald.

Simplicity is the key to designing good characters. Many times, the most amazing character turns out to be the simplest to construct. You should always think about your character's construction and try to keep your models simple and light. Simple characters also animate faster and easier. If your character has too many parts or more detail than he needs, you will have more problems to keep track of when animating. Problems that slow you or your system down will detract from your creative processes and cause your animation to suffer.

Good design means knowing your software. This dog has lots of hair, which requires custom software to create.

Without the custom hair software, the dog becomes a different character.

This character is very simple, but still can be animated quite effectively.

Even a character with no body, like this sun, can have lots of character.

Categories of Design

Designs fall into two broad categories: realistic and stylized. Realistic designs try to mimic reality. If this is the case, you need to design your character in accordance with nature. Stylized designs are caricatures of reality and give you far more design choices.

Realistic Designs

Digital character animation has been very successful in the area of special effects for feature films. Computer animators and special effects teams have been able to make characters, such as dinosaurs, look completely real and integrate them into live-action environments. Many of the larger studios are working toward creating digital humans, and I'm sure they will succeed. Digital stuntmen have already been employed to complete stunts that were too expensive or impossible for a real stuntman to do.

If you want to create characters that closely mimic reality, digital animation is the medium you should choose. I must warn you that reality is a hard thing to simulate, regardless of medium. Creating an effective animation of a realistic character requires a thorough knowledge of anatomy and motion.

Audiences expect realistic characters such as this to move realistically.

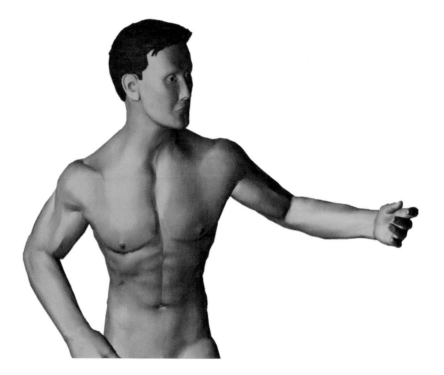

If you want to design and animate a realistic character, reference of the real thing is essential. In traditional animation, many of the large studios have been known to bring animals to the studio for the animators to study. If you can't afford to hire an ostrich or an elephant for the afternoon, a trip to the zoo or a videotape of a nature documentary can provide equally good reference. If you want to create a realistic human, a trip to the zoo could also be in order. Of course, for humans, our cities are our zoos. In a big city, this means stepping out your front door and watching the passersby.

Stylized Designs

Creating a caricatured world is usually more fun and gives you much more freedom in your designs. Computer animation can mimic reality, but animation is always at its best when it goes far beyond reality. Think of those classic cartoons from the 1940s. Daffy Duck was a wild and wacky character, but he was a duck. In real life, ducks swim, eat, and breed, but that's about it. Ducks certainly don't talk, and they don't hold grudges against smart-aleck rabbits. It's way beyond the realm of reality, but a talking duck is still entertaining. The audience will accept the animated universe as you, the animator, define it. If your character pulls off his head and dribbles it like a basketball—we don't question, we simply laugh.

The audience's preconceptions are important. If your audience sees a picture-perfect digital human on the screen, it will expect him to walk, talk, and act like a human. If he's the slightest bit off from the way a real human acts, the illusion is lost. If you give the audience a caricatured cartoon hedgehog, however, there are absolutely no preconceptions. The audience will be much more accepting of your character, and you, as the animator, will have the freedom to make him move and act however you want—even if it's not exactly the way a real hedgehog would act.

A stylized character such as this cartoon cat may be easier to design and animate than a realistic human.

A caricatured design, however, is not a license to animate your characters poorly. Good animation makes even the simplest character appear to breathe. A simple box can be animated quite easily by twisting, turning, and moving it about so that it has weight, volume, and personality. The most important thing about a character is the personality and whether that personality engages the audience.

Designing a Character

A character's design depends largely on the character and its personality. Your character's design should also be an indication of its personality and its role in the film. A character who's big and mean will have broad shoulders and beady eyes. One with big eyes and a potbelly will seem meek in comparison. A character with lots of big muscles and a very small head might appear a bit clueless, and the character with a huge head and no muscles might appear to be a genius.

Of course, these examples are stereotypes, and it is often a good idea to play against type. A good example might be a large, threatening character who has a small voice and timid personality. Design can also drive the personality of a character. A duck born with no feathers might be driven by his inadequacy to corner the market in down pillows, for example.

Head and Body Proportions

When deciding on the height of your character, use the size of the head as the guide. An average human is about 6 to 8 heads tall. If the character is taller, it may appear more lithe and graceful.

A realistic character is between 6 and 8 heads tall.

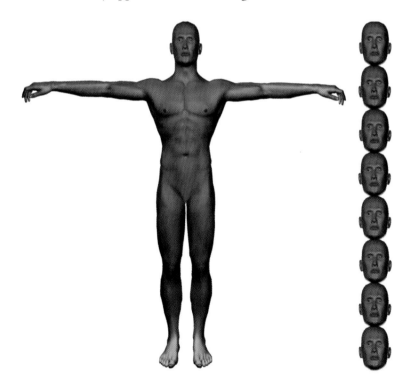

Cartoon characters, on the other hand, can have much bigger heads in relation to the body. Mr. Potato Head, in fact, has no body, he's simply a giant head with arms and feet. If your character has a body, it may be only as large the head itself. A larger head in proportion to the body tends to make a character look cute. Many characters are only 2 or 3 heads tall.

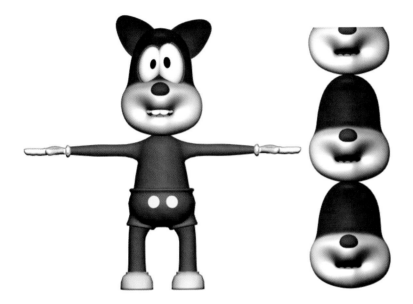

This cartoon character is a little more than 2 heads tall. The bigger the head in relation to the body, the cuter the character will look.

Eyes

The size of the eyes in relation to the face determines how we perceive a character. If the eyes are small and beady, the character may appear mean or angry. Big eyes convey innocence and look cute. Placement of the eyes also plays a huge role in the character. If the eyes are low on the head, the character seems older and more brainy with a bigger fore-head. Placing the eyes higher on the head tends to make the character look younger.

The eyes of your character can also change shape. If your character has cartoon eyes, you can bend and flex the eyes wildly with the character's emotions. If your character has eyes that are inside the head, and more realistic, you don't have as much freedom in changing the shape at ani-mation time. If you want the eyes bigger than normal, you need to model them big at the beginning.

The shape of your character's eyes can also determine its personality. Round, symmetrical eyes can look pleasant, though a slight bit of asymmetry will add realism and character.

Eyes that are wildly asymmetrical can make your character look like he's begging for neurons.

Narrow eyes, such as these, can give a character a more devious look.

Feet

On real humans, feet are relatively small in relation to the body. Your foot should be almost exactly as long as your forearm. Many times your character will be wearing shoes. In this case, it is not necessary to model feet to place inside the shoes, the shoes can simply attach to the legs at the ankles.

A cartoon character, on the other hand, may have the feet exaggerated so that they are much larger than normal. If you decide to exaggerate the feet, remember that your character still needs to walk. Feet that are slightly longer than the legs can be animated using a number of tricks, such as walking with a waddle or scaling the legs as the feet pass under the body. Feet that are a lot longer than the legs will prove difficult, if not impossible, to animate.

This stylized character has feet that are bigger than normal.

Too big, however, and he'll have problems walking.

Hands

Like feet, hands on a stylized character can be slightly oversized to give it a cartoonish look. If your design is more realistic, you might want to proportion the hands realistically as well. If realism is the goal, you may need to attach your hands seamlessly to the forearm. This may mean building your character as one solid mesh or using an advanced seam-hiding technique, such as a blend, to keep the skin smooth. These techniques are described later.

Here we have a character whose hand and body are one seamless mesh.

If you want, you can give your character cartoon gloves for hands. In the 1920s, cartoon gloves were devised by animators so that hands and wrists would be easier to draw.

The design stuck, mostly because it looks stylish and it works. For a 3D animator, cartoon gloves serve much the same purpose. They can be much easier to attach than a naked hand, because the glove can have a seam where it attaches.

A cartoon glove is stylish, and it helps you design around the tricky problem of seamlessly attaching your character's hand to the wrist.

Clothing and Other Accessories

Clothes make the man, or so they say. If your character is an astronaut, he will probably be wearing a space suit. A caveman may need only a bearskin. Clothing tells the audience, to a large degree, who the character is and how he should be perceived. If you want a character to be mean and nasty, dress him accordingly. This doesn't mean that every villain you create needs to wear black, however. When designing characters and their clothing, try to be original and avoid stereotypes.

Do clothes make the man? The character on the left may be perceived differently than the one on the right, simply because of his clothes.

Clothing that behaves like real fabric, however, will require custom software, which may affect your design decisions.

Clothing can also help you design around the limitations of your modeler. If you model your character in a manner that forces you to place a seam at its waist, a belt may be a good way to hide this. A dress or a long shirt can help hide the hip area, which can be difficult to model and animate with some software. Clothing that behaves like real fabric, however, requires custom software, which may affect your design decisions.

Clothes may also be used to hide seams. This character seems well dressed.

The shirt hides the seams at the arms and neck, and the pants hide the seams for the feet.

This character has an unsightly seam at his waist.

Add a belt and the audience will never see the seam.

Designing Your Own Characters

Now that you have a bit of information under your belt, you can start designing your own characters. How you realize your designs depends on your skills and abilities. Some people like to draw, others like to sculpt, and some like to work directly with the computer.

Designing on Paper

The simplest way to design your characters is to sketch them on paper. A pencil is a wonderful thing, because it enables you to very quickly block out the size and shape of your character. If you know how to write your name, you can most likely draw a character.

If you've spent any amount of time modeling characters on the computer, you'll develop a visual sense that will translate to paper as well. It seems that modeling characters improves your drawing, and drawing characters improves your modeling. Another way to improve both skills is through a life drawing class. This is the single best way to aesthetically understand the human form.

Regardless of your skills, after you've got a few sketches of your character, you can use them as reference for modeling the character. Many people, however, need a more precise guide. This is particularly true when you need to model an existing character, such as the latest comic book hero who's appearing in your company's new video game.

In these cases, you need to draw several accurate views of your character. Usually, this means a minimum of a front view and a side view. When drawing these views, make sure to draw the character with its arms outstretched. This is the standard way of modeling characters, because it makes mesh deformation a lot easier. The final drawings are then scanned into the computer, where they are used as reference.

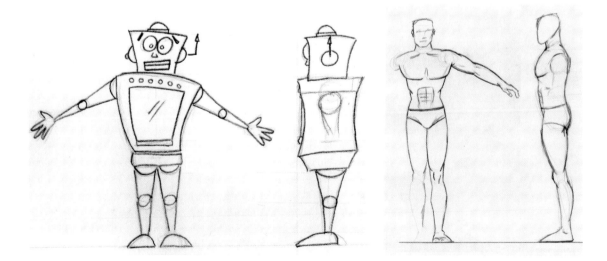

However your character is designed, it's a good idea to make an accurate drawing before starting the modeling process.

Using Images as Reference

There are several techniques for using your drawings as reference. Most commonly, the scans are simply used as a background image. This means configuring your software so that the image takes up the viewport of your modeling program, enabling you to trace the contours of the image.

Another way is to create a simple object, such as a plane or a thin box that has the images applied as texture maps. This allows you to model more interactively, because you can move the camera to get custom views of the character as it's being modeled.

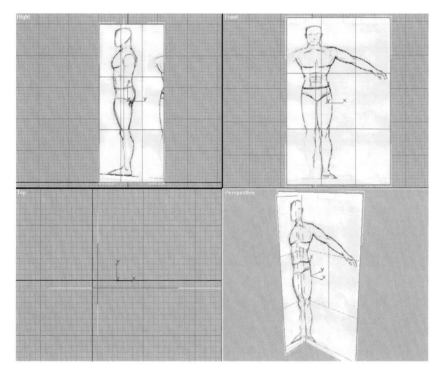

After the drawing is scanned into the computer, it can be mapped to a series of planes, which act as references when modeling.

The final, and very old-fashioned, way is not to scan the image, but to use a digitizing tablet to trace the drawing. This method does work, but it is certainly far from interactive.

Designing in Clay

Another way to design characters is to sculpt them in clay. A three-dimensional clay sculpture is much closer to the final character than any two-dimensional drawing can be. Clay, however, is much messier, and certainly a great deal more time-consuming.

Like drawing, sculpting is an art. There are plenty of books and classes available to teach the finer points of sculpture. Those who understand 3D modeling should take to sculpture quite easily. You will probably find that the interactivity of clay is far superior to any computer-driven interface.

As with drawings, a proper sculpture used for modeling characters should be in a neutral pose. The arms should be outstretched with the palms forward and the legs slightly apart. It's always tempting to sculpt your character in a dynamic pose. Although it may make a nice sculpture, don't succumb to this temptation—it will cause you nothing but headaches. If your character is sculpted properly, in a neutral pose, your digital character will be able to hit any pose you desire.

Using Sculpey

Most people who realize their designs as sculpture tend to use Sculpey. Sculpey is a soft polymer clay that can be baked to a hard finish in a conventional oven rather than a kiln. This makes it much more accessible for the average person.

There are several types of Sculpey. The original Sculpey is a plain white clay, and is the least expensive. For most purposes it is perfectly fine, but it's prone to cracking over time. Super Sculpey is more durable, and Sculpey III comes in designer colors. Which one you choose depends on your requirements. For character models that are disposable, Sculpey is more than adequate. Those wanting to keep their sculptures forever may want to invest in the higher-quality lines.

Sculpey is a soft clay, so it's best used with a bit of support. This means creating an armature, or a skeleton, for your character out of wire or aluminum foil. This skeleton will help support the clay until it is baked.

In addition to supporting your character, creating a skeleton out of wire and aluminum foil enables you to use less Sculpey. Not only does it save you money, but it makes the curing process much easier. Sculpey needs to be baked at 275 degrees Fahrenheit (130 degrees Centigrade) for 15 minutes per quarter-inch of thickness. If your character is made out of pure Sculpey, it will take a 4-inch–thick character 4 hours to bake, which means your outer layers will probably singe and burn long before the center is fully cooked. Always try to keep the Sculpey less than an inch thick. After Sculpey is cured, it forms a very tough finish. Even a half-inch–thick character can be sanded quite vigorously without breaking, though you should always be careful. For decoration, Sculpey can also be painted with standard acrylics.

Getting Sculpture into the Computer

After you create an acceptable sculpture, there are two methods for getting it into the computer for modeling. The first method is to simply take a photograph of the sculpture and scan it into the computer. The second method is to digitize the actual surface of the model, using a 3D scanner or digitizer. The one you choose depends on your needs and also your budget.

Photographing Sculpture

The simplest and cheapest way to get your sculpture into the computer is to take photographs of it at several different angles. Typically, a front view and a side view will suffice, but extra detail may need more angles. Just as with drawings, these photographs can then be scanned into the computer and used as reference for modeling.

When photographing a model, try not to use a short focal length, or "fish-eye" lens on your camera. This will distort the image, making modeling difficult. You should also try to light the model so that the contour of the sculpture is apparent. A washed-out photograph provides very little useful information.

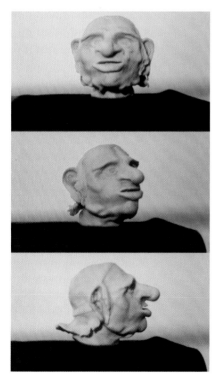

Photographing a sculpture is an easy way to get it into a computer. Take several different views of your character.

(Sculpture by Tuong Nguyen)

Photography can also be used as reference for real-world items. A photograph of a toy, an animal, or even a human can work just as effectively as a photograph of a sculpture.

The photograph can then be scanned into the computer and used as reference, just as with a drawing.

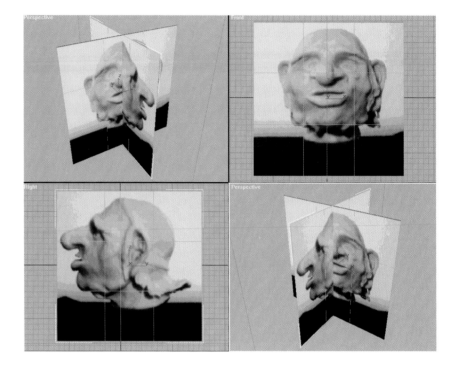

Digitizing Sculpture

The second, and more complex, method is to digitize or scan the model. There are a number of digitizing devices on the market, which range from small mechanical digitizers to human-sized laser scanners. There are also many service bureaus that can do the work for those without the money to purchase such expensive equipment.

There are two main ways of digitizing a sculpture. The first method, employed by most laser-based systems, scans the model in a grid-like fashion. This creates a dense cloud of points, which duplicates the surface quite accurately. Unfortunately, such a dense model will not animate with any degree of control. The dense model must be brought into the modeling package and used as a three-dimensional reference. From there, the animatable model is built by snapping vertices to the surface of the reference.

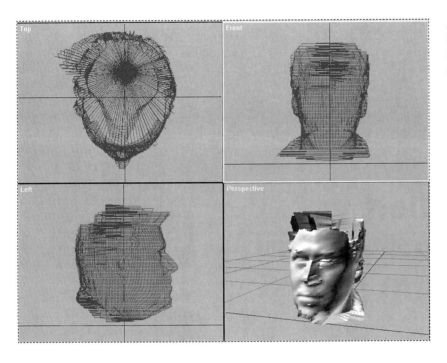

A laser scan creates a model that is both dense and grid-like. The scan must be used as reference for creating a model that can be animated.

Mechanical digitizers can also scan clouds of points, but most of the hand-operated ones enable you to specify exactly which points are digitized. This makes it possible to draw out the topology of your wireframe directly on the sculpture. The detail can then be digitized very precisely, practically modeling the character as you digitize.

Exercise #1: Character Design

In this first exercise, you design a simple character. First, think about what type of character you want to create. Is it real or stylized? What are that character's major personality traits? When you have a good idea of who your character is, take a pencil and paper and sketch some character designs that you might want to model in the next few chapters. (If you're more familiar with sculpting, you might want to do this in clay.) These designs should focus on the outward appearance of the character and its proportions, and also tell the viewer a bit about its personality—whether the character is small, large, skinny, fat, timid, aggressive, and so on.

When you have a number of designs, go through each character and think of how that character might be constructed in your chosen software. You are just getting started, so these issues may not be readily apparent. Your design may change as you learn more about how to build characters. This will be discussed in the next few chapters.

CHAPTER 2

Modeling Basics

When a character has been designed, it needs to be built. This means translating the design into a 3D model that can be animated. Building a character in the computer is called modeling. This takes the basic design of the character and turns it into a 3D model that can then be manipulated. The basic decisions of how a character will be modeled affect the entire animation process.

When modeled, the character must not only look good, it must animate well. This means that the surface of the character can deform easily and quickly for fast manipulation. A character that can be manipulated in real-time makes animation a breeze. Building and configuring your character properly before you ever start animating saves you many headaches in the long run.

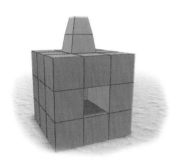

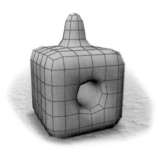

Surface Types

When modeling, you can use many different surfaces to create a character. These include polygons, patches, and NURBS-based surfaces. In addition to these three basic types, there are also other types of surfaces, such as metaballs, membranes, and hierarchical patches, to name but a few. If you understand the basics of polygons, patches, and NURBS (Non-Uniform Rational B-Splines), however, you'll have the basics that will enable you to work in almost any package.

The surface you choose for constructing your character depends on a number of factors. Some of this decision is software-driven. If your software supports only polygonal surfaces, for example, your decision is already made—the character must be built out of polygons. Another factor may be the number of tools, meaning that some packages are more adept at one type of modeling over another. A package may simply have more tools to manipulate NURBS surfaces, which might make NURBS the appropriate choice for the character. For those packages that support a variety of surface types, the decision comes down to the demands of the project, the individual characters, and, of course, personal preference.

Some characters lend themselves quite nicely to polygonal surfaces, and others may be approached via a patch-based or NURBS-based modeling method. A character in a gaming environment, for example, may need to be polygonal simply because the game engine supports only polygons. Characters made for high-resolution output, such as film, typically are modeled as NURBS surfaces. Patches and subdivided polygonal surfaces, however, are catching up in offering the capability of deforming and can be even better for quick interaction within the software.

The best way to make the best decision is to understand all the surface types equally. This involves working with all the different geometry types and trying your hand at modeling and animating a character with each. Of course, after you've worked with the different surface types for a while, you'll develop your own preferences, which will affect your future decisions. Also be alert for new methods and technologies—the world of 3D animation is hardly standing still.

Polygonal Surfaces

Polygonal modeling was the first form of modeling developed for computer graphics, and, because it is the most fundamental form of modeling, it still holds up quite well. All other forms of modeling resolve to polygons at one point or another, because no matter what modeling tool you use, most software turns your model into polygons before rendering. Polygons are simply triangles or rectangles, each representing a plane and defining a small area of the character's surface.

A big benefit to polygonal modeling is in the number of different surface types that can be defined. Many NURBS-based and patch-based modelers are limited to surfaces that are topologically simple, such as a cylinder or a sphere. In order to create an object that's more complex, such as a body, you may need to make it out of several surfaces that are seamed together. Polygons don't suffer from this topological conundrum, and with a polygonal modeler, you're free to make your surface as complex as you desire.

Polygonal models have three basic elements: the vertex, the edge, and the polygon. Essentially, these elements represent the three dimensions. A vertex is a single point, an edge is a line connecting two vertices, and a polygon is a surface defined by three edges or vertices. Polygons can have more than three sides, however, and many packages allow as many sides as you want to define a polygon, though internally these many-sided polygons are resolved to triangles when rendered.

The big gripe that people have with polygonal surfaces is that, in order to get a reasonably smooth surface, the surface needs to have lots and lots of polygons. When animating, however, a high-resolution polygonal model is the last thing you'd ever want to work with. It's slow to deform, and tears easily.

The way around this problem is to model a low-resolution polygonal model that animates easily, and then use techniques to add the extra detail needed for a smooth surface at render-time. As you will see later, this technique is called subdivision surfaces, and it can produce excellent results.

Patch Surfaces

A patch is a surface that has curves for edges. These curves, in turn, define a curved surface. Curves come in a variety of flavors, as do the associated patches. Curves can be called by a number of different names, such as linear, cardinal, B-spline and Bézier, but they also can be named by their degree.

The degree of the curve refers to the mathematical formula used to represent it. The higher the degree of the curve, the more calculation you need to create it. The easiest way to remember the order of the curve is that the degree of the curve is one less than the number of points required to define the curve. Therefore, a first-degree curve needs two points to define it, a second-degree curve needs three points, and so on. Some packages allow different degrees of curves to be combined to make patches—for example with those that are linear along the U direction, and B-spline curves along the V direction.

A linear curve looks like a series of lines connecting the control points. The curves defining the surface are equivalent to the edges in a polygonal surface.

A cardinal is a curve that passes through the control points. Each point also has a tangent control.

A B-spline curve rarely passes through its control points, and having the control points far away can make manipulating a surface a bit confusing.

A Bézier curve is similar to those used in popular drawing programs, such as Adobe Illustrator. The curve passes through each control point, and each point has two tangential controls for adjusting the weight of the curve on either side of the vertex.

NURBS Surfaces

NURBS are really just an extension of the B-spline patch described previously. The extension—and the big difference—with a NURBS surface is the term non-uniform. This means that each vertex can also be weighted to affect the curvature of the surface more precisely. Weighting also enables a simpler surface, because fewer points are needed to define the same surface.

In many cases, NURBS can be manipulated in much the same way as other types of patches. A number of tools have also been developed specifically for NURBS surfaces. As you will see later in this chapter, these include the capability of creating curves on a surface, plus the capability of trimming surfaces and blending between these curves.

Modeling Strategies

With a number of different surface types, the choice of surface depends on any number of factors. Whichever surface type you choose, there are a few strategies you can use.

Keep It Light

Although the type of surfaces you use is decided by a number of factors, the resulting model ideally should be able to be manipulated as fast as you can animate it. The last thing you want to be confronted with when animating is waiting a few seconds (even a fraction of a second) for the screen to up-date each time you pose the character. The most important feedback an animator can get is the ability to scrub the animation in real-time as it's keyframed.

This means you need to keep your characters light. The term "keep it light" means to make the most with each and every vertex, spline, edge, and patch in your model. If you model your character with exactly the right detail, it will remain light. This will make animation easier simply because there will be less vertices to calculate when moving the surface of the character around—speeding up interaction and making the animator's life easier. Having exactly the right amount of detail also enables smoother deformation of the surface, because it significantly reduces the possibility of tearing and breaking.

Mixing and Matching Surface Types

There also may be times in which one type of surface may be great for the body, but another is more applicable to the hands or face. Many times, it's acceptable to create a character in segments. If this is the case, these segments can be constructed out of the surface most appropriate for the task at hand.

Modeling Basics

Before you start modeling, you need to familiarize yourself with the tools. The next few sections go over the basic tools found in the majority of software packages. Many packages may have more tools; some will have less. By familiarizing yourself with the basics, however, you should be able to get up to speed on any software fairly quickly.

One problem when discussing modeling tools is that, many times, there is confusion over terms. Three different software packages can call the same tool by three different names. In these cases, I provide a glossary table to cross-reference the term defined for this book with the terms used in the major packages.

Basics of Polygonal Modeling

Polygonal modeling can create excellent characters, and many packages are still strictly polygon-based. This is by no means a bad thing, because a good polygonal modeler enables you to sculpt a surface almost as if it were made out of clay. Polygonal modeling also affords a great degree of topological freedom not found in many patch-based modelers.

The fundamentals of polygonal modeling are fairly simple. Polygonal models consist of three basic elements: the vertex, the edge, and the polygon. There are a number of ways you can manipulate these elements. These manipulations are listed in Table 2.1.

Vertices

Vertices represent a single point in space and are one-dimensional objects. Two vertices can be connected to create edges. Some modelers enable additional operations, such as the capability of extruding and beveling a vertex, both of which add extra edges and polygons.

Edges

Edges are defined by two vertices. When viewing an object in wireframe mode, you are seeing the edges. In effect, edges are lines and are two-dimensional objects. When three or more edges are connected, they create a polygon. There are a number of operations that can be performed on an edge. These include extruding and beveling, which again add extra edges and polygons. A collapse operation eliminates the edge, reducing it to a single vertex.

Polygons

Polygons are defined by three or more edges. In effect, polygons are planes and are three-dimensional objects. In order for an object to render, polygons are required. Most packages enable a polygon to have more than three sides, but these are generally tesselated to triangles when rendering time rolls around.

There are a number of operations that can be performed on a polygon. Collapsing a polygon removes the polygon, collapsing it to a single vertex. Extruding, insetting, and beveling are all variations of the same operation, creating one extra polygon per edge of the original polygon. The difference is in how the original polygon is handled. In an extrude, it is moved outward or inward, typically along the normal (that is, at a right angle to the face of the polygon). In an inset, the original polygon is scaled, typically inward, along the surface of the original polygon. The bevel is a combination of the two, both moving and scaling the original polygon.

Table 2.1

Basics of Polygonal Modeling

Polygonal Models Consist of Vertices, Edges, and Polygons

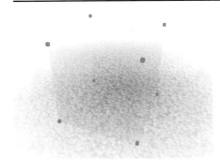

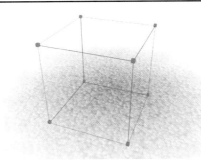

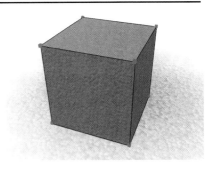

Vertex—A vertex is a single point in space.

Edge—Two connected vertices form an edge, which is also a line.

Polygon—Three or more connected edges make a polygon, which is a plane.

Operations Performed on Vertices

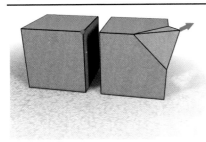

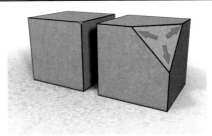

Extrude—Pulls the vertex outward and adds three polygons.

Bevel—Expands the vertex to a polygon along the edges.

Operations Performed on Edges

Extrude—An extruded edge creates a new polygon along the edge's normal.

Bevel—Beveling an edge creates a new face.

continues

Continued

Basics of Polygonal Modeling

Operations Performed on Edges

Collapse—Deletes the edge, creating a single vertex.

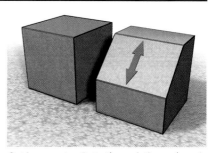

Cut/connect—Cuts the existing edges in half, and then connects with an edge.

Operations Performed on Polygons

Extrude—Pulls the face in or out along the normal, adding four new polygons.

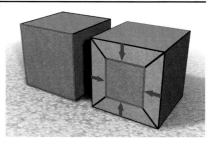

Inset—Shrinks the polygon along its plane, adding four new polygons.

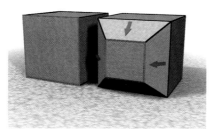

Bevel—An extrude with an inset. Four new polygons are added.

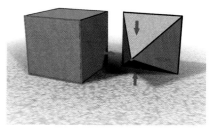

Collapse—Deletes the polygon, creating a single vertex.

Polygonal Modeling Techniques

When the basic operations are known, modeling with polygons is relatively straightforward and simple. Typically, a basic shape is created, such as a box, cylinder, or sphere. This basic object is then modified through a number of techniques to create a more complex shape for your character.

Start Simple

When modeling polygonal surfaces, or any surface for that matter, it's always best to start with a small amount of surface detail and work your way up to higher amounts of detail. Most polygonal modelers start with a simple primitive, such as a box or a sphere, and add detail, working and shaping the surface as needed.

The mantra for modeling is to make the most with the least amount of detail. People who model for interactive games have it particularly rough, because their models have to be incredibly light. If you want a lesson in simple, but effective, modeling, sit with a game modeler for a few hours.

Edge Loops

One of the more important things to master when learning to model with polygons is the concept of the edge loop. An edge loop is a ring of edges that define an area of the character. In the face, edge loops are used to define the mouth, brows, and eye sockets. In a body, they determine the outline of the torso, arms, and legs.

One way to mentally picture edge loops is to think of a map that has contours that represent the elevation of the surface. The contours are continuous loops of elevation. If a map such as this is brought into a 3D package and the contours traced with edge loops, the map takes shape.

Typically, an edge loop is created by cutting two existing edges in half and connecting them to create a new edge. The way these edges are cut determines a great deal about how the resulting model behaves. When opposite edges of a rectangular polygon are cut and connected, the result is two four-sided, or quadratic, polygons. When connecting adjacent edges, you get a triangular and a five-sided polygon, which can prove to be a problem when the character deforms. It is always best to create quadratics, because they tend to deform more predictably than a triangular surface; so when sketching out an edge loop, try to avoid connecting adjacent corners.

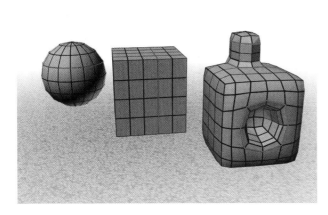

An edge loop, highlighted in red, is simply a continuous loop of edges that define the contours of the model.

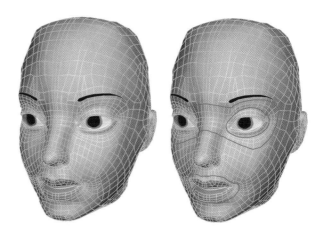

Even the contours of a model as complex as a face have recognizable contours defined by edge loops. The contours of the mouth and eyes, for example, can be defined by concentric loops.

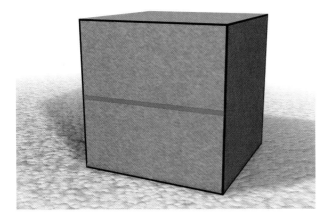

When opposite edges of a rectangular polygon are cut and connected, the result is two four-sided, or quadratic, polygons.

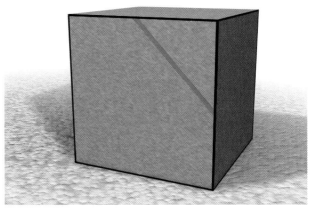

When connecting adjacent edges, you get a triangular and a five-sided polygon, which can prove problematic when the character deforms.

Subdivision Surfaces

Not everyone models for interactive games, and most people who model for film or video want their models looking as smooth and natural as possible. At first, this may seem to be a difficult problem, because the extra detail can prove to be difficult to manage. Fortunately, with the right tools, a properly constructed low-resolution model can become a high-resolution model almost automatically. This automatic technique, subdivision surfaces, is called a variety of names by various software vendors.

Polygons Become Patches

When you subdivide a polygonal surface, the software adds detail. It first needs to figure out where to place all the added detail. These extra polygons are placed according to any number of formulas. The theory of these tools is simple: The three or four points that define the edge of a polygon are just that—points in space. By interpolating these points along a curve rather than a straight line, you can approximate the same effects of patch modeling.

The simplest way of calculating this extra detail is by cutting some corners—literally. A woodcarver sculpting a block of wood starts by whittling off the corners of the block. If you can find a way to mathematically whittle off the corners of your virtual character, you would get a smoother surface. This technique is called corner clipping.

Corner clipping takes the midpoints, or centers, of your object's polygons and connects them with intermediate polygons, turning one polygon into four, four into sixteen, and so on. Each time this is done, the corners get whittled away, and the object gets smoother. The interesting thing about corner clipping is that, when the clipping is repeated to infinity, the surface becomes exactly the same as a B-spline patch.

In Other Words...

Subdivision surfaces have been around for quite a while, and, as usual, many vendors have adopted their own terms for the technique, most commonly dubbed smoothing:

Houdini—Smoothing

LightWave—MetaNurbs and Metaform

MAX—MeshSmooth, Tesselate, and third-party plug-ins, such as Infografica's SurfReyes

Maya—Smoothing

Nichimen—Smoothing

Softimage—Rounding

trueSpace—Nurbs

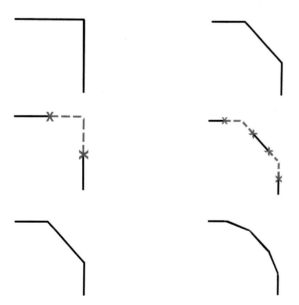

Subdividing two lines is simple. Take two simple lines, find the midpoints, and then cut the corners.

Repeating this step further refines the lines so that they approach the outline of a B-spline curve.

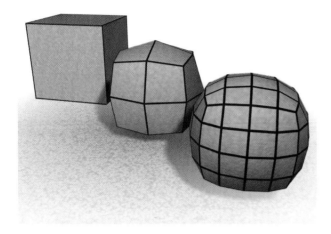

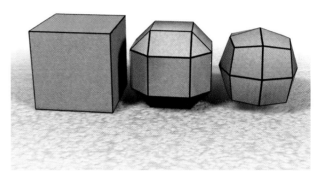

For surfaces, the theory is the same, but each face is subdivided. This smooths the surface.

Smoothing can be configured to produce a mixture of trangular and quadratic polygons

Let's wait a second while that last statement sinks in. Mathematically, a smoothed polygonal surface is exactly the same as a B-spline patch. The next time some wacko tells you that patches are better than polygons, just remind him or her of this little tidbit.

Of course, infinity is a pretty big number, even for a computer, so for most purposes, we need to only approximate infinity. Usually, only two or three rounds of smoothing are required to get a low-res polygonal surface to look perfectly smooth on a film or video screen.

Subdivision Surfaces and Animation

The one problem with a character who's been subdivided is that the extra detail that subdivision creates also weighs down the character. This makes speedy interaction and deformation nearly impossible. This is resolved through a number of tricks. Most of these center around the simple task of creating the subdivision surface after the character is animated and before it is rendered.

Some object-oriented packages, such as 3D Studio MAX, LightWave, and Houdini enable you to subdivide the surface at any point in the animation process. Typically, this is after the character is deformed and after it is animated.

Most of these packages enable you to switch the subdivision modifier on and off. When the modifier is turned off, the character is low-resolution and animates quickly. When subdivision is turned on, the character becomes high-resolution for rendering. Because the subdivision happens after deformation of the low-res model, the smoothing does not exhibit any tears or creases.

Other packages, such as Nichimen and LightWave, enable this task to happen automatically at render-time. Essentially, this performs the same function as in the previous example.

Another way to perform this task is to keep both a high-and a low-resolution model handy. The low-resolution model is animated. The animation curves are then copied to the high-resolution model and rendered. The one problem with this method is that, because they are separate models, the deformation on the low-res character may not exactly match the high-res character, causing possible tears and other small errors.

When animating using subdivision surfaces, animate the low-res model for speedy interaction (right). For high-quality output, subdivide after deformation and before rendering (left).

Booleans Are Evil

Yes, that's right, they're just plain evil. Many polygonal modeling packages have a Boolean feature, which enables you to add and subtract surfaces quite easily. This might be nice for solid objects, but not for those that need to deform.

When a Boolean operation is applied to an object, it creates tons of useless polygons. If you observe the seam created from a Boolean operation, you'll notice a huge amount of tiny faces used to bridge inaccuracies in the fusing of the models. These polygons add very little to the model, but can nearly double or triple the weight.

A Boolean operation quickly enables you to add and subtract surfaces, such as this cylinder from the sphere.

Unfortunately, when the object is sub-divided, the Boolean surface breaks up because of unwanted artifacts.

Instead of using Booleans, select the faces and use them to model the detail needed. This results in a perfectly clean surface that subdivides well.

Even worse, if you're using Booleans to model a low-resolution charac-ter, the seam gives you all sorts of trouble. A subdivided Boolean opera-tion looks like a bad surgery scar. This might appear good if you're modeling Frankenstein, but even then you want total control over how your model behaves when subdivided, so just avoid Booleans.

Instead of Booleans, smart polygonal modelers rely on the standard toolkit for polygonal modeling. If you need to create a branch, bevel or extrude polygons outward. If you want to cut a hole in an object, bevel or extrude inward. This way, the edges are clean and smooth, with no problems.

Basics of Patch Modeling

Patch modeling is another excellent way to create characters. Patches are surfaces defined by curves, such as linear, cardinal, B-spline, or Bézier. Typically, these surfaces are four-sided, or a conglomeration of individual four-sided surfaces. As stated previously, curves and surfaces are defined by their degree, which is the amount of control you have over the surface (see Table 2.2):

- Linear—A first-degree curve, this looks like a series of lines con-necting the control points. The curves defining the surface are equivalent to the edges in a polygonal surface.

- Cardinal—A second-degree curve, this curve passes through the control points. Each point has a tangent control as well. As you can see, a patch created with cardinal curves has four rows of vertices in each direction, for a total of sixteen points. The control points also extend beyond the edge of the surface. This is needed because cardinals do not have true endpoint interpolation, and the extra points define the curve.

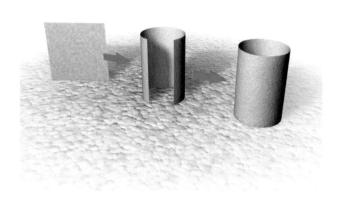

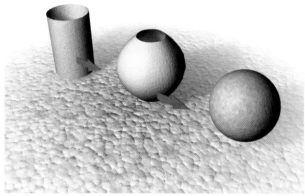

A single patch can cover only a surface that is regular, or has no branches. A patch can be wrapped into a cylinder.

Pinch up the ends to get a sphere.

■ B-spline—A third-degree curve, this type of curve rarely passes through its control points, and having the control points far away can make manipulating a surface a bit confusing. In this type of curve, the extra points are called knots. As with a cardinal curve, B-splines do not interpolate beyond the endpoints. This means extra points are needed beyond the edges of the patch to define its curvature.

■ Bézier—Also a third-degree curve, this curve is similar to those used in popular drawing programs, such as Adobe Illustrator. The curve passes through each control point, and each point has two tangential controls for adjusting the weight of the curve on either side of the vertex. These extra controls enable endpoint interpolation, so the points are at the edges of the patch.

One nice thing about Béziers is that the extra control points enable a wide range of control over the curvature, from a smooth surface to a sharp crease. Another nice thing is that this control is localized, so changes to one part of the model do not affect other parts.

Regular Surfaces

The easiest surface to create with a patch is to a regular surface. This is a smooth surface that is basically a single patch. Single patch models can be made by modifying primitives, such as a sphere for a head or a cylinder for a body.

One advantage with regular surfaces is that they texture quite easily. The U and V lines of the surface will map directly to the X and Y coordinates of an image. If you can create an object using one regular surface, you do not have to apply mapping coordinates to the surface, as you would with an irregular polygonal surface.

When modeling with patches, think of a regular surface as a giant piece of wrapping paper. Anything you can wrap with a single sheet of paper, you can create as a regular surface. To create a cylinder, simply roll the paper in a circle. To create a sphere, pinch up the ends of the paper.

Creating Patches from Curves

When creating a patch-based surface, one way to easily define the surface is to sketch out the shape with curves. After the basics of the shape are defined, tools are used to turn those curves into surfaces (see Table 2.2):

- Extrude—Extrude works by sweeping a profile curve along a straight line or a path. This creates a shape that is essentially a cylinder.

- Lathe/Revolve—A lathe or a revolve takes an outline curve and sweeps it around an axis to create a surface. The resulting surface may be either a cylinder or be closed at one or more poles, like a sphere.

- Lofting—Lofting is similar to extrude but enables you to have multiple outlines along the path. This can give you much better control of the shape.

- Skinning—Also known as a U-loft or a V-loft, skinning is closely related to lofting and enables multiple curves to be used to generate a surface.

- Ruled—Ruled uses two curves to define opposite edges of the surface. It is similar to skinning, but the surface is built along the curve rather than perpendicular to it.

- Boundary surfaces—Boundary surfaces take three or four curves and use them to define the edges of a patch.

- BiRail—BiRail constructs a surface by sweeping one or two profile curves along two rail curves. If one profile is selected, the tool works much like an extrude or loft. If two curves are selected, the tool works more like a boundary surface.

Table 2.2

Basics of Patch and NURBS Modeling

Basic Types of Surfaces

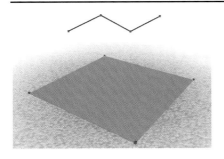

Linear—A first-degree curve, this looks like a series of lines connecting the control points.

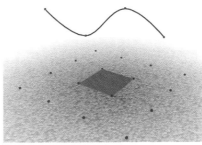

Cardinal—A second-degree curve, this curve passes through the control points. The patch has vertices beyond the edges.

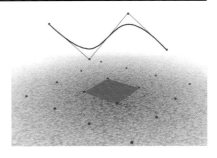

B-spline—A third-degree curve, this type of curve rarely passes through its control points. The patch has vertices beyond the edges.

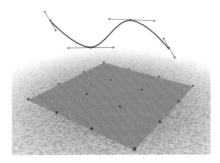

Bézier—The curve passes through each control point, and each point has two tangential controls for adjusting the weight of the curve on either side of the vertex.

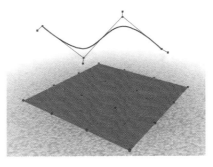

NURBS—A nonrational form of the B-spline, this curve has weights to adjust the tangency.

Basic Patch Operations

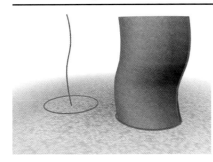

Extrude—Extrude works by sweeping a profile curve along a straight line or a path.

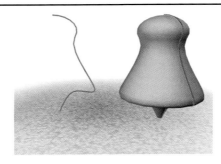

Lathe/revolve—A lathe or revolve takes an outline curve and sweeps it around an axis to create a surface.

continues

Continued

Basics of Patch and NURBS Modeling

Basic Patch Operations

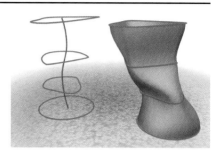

Skin—Also known as a U-loft or a V-loft, skinning is closely related to lofting and enables multiple curves to be used to generate a surface.

Loft—Lofting is similar to extrude, but enables you to have multiple outlines along the path.

Advanced Patch Operations

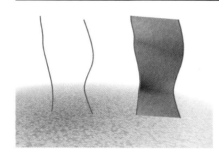

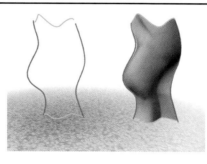

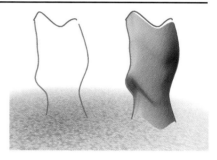

Ruled—Uses two curves to define opposite edges of the surface.

Boundary surfaces—These take three or four curves and use them to define the edges of a patch.

BiRail—Constructs a surface by sweeping one or two profile curves along two rail curves.

NURB Curve Operations

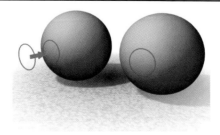

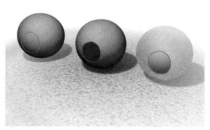

Curve on surface—A curve on surface can be created by projecting it (right) or drawing it directly on the surface (left).

Trims—A trim can be used to cut out the area inside a curve on surface (middle) or outside a curve on surface (left).

NURB Surface Operations

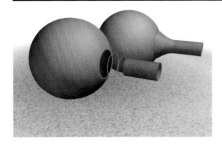

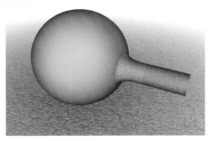

Loft—To connect a curve on surface to another surface, use the curve as the base for a loft or skinning operation.

Blend—A blend creates a similar surface that automatically changes shape to maintain tangency.

Fillet—A fillet is a blend that maintains a concave semicircular outline.

Chamfer—A chamfer rounds off the corners of a surface.

Stitching Patches Together

There are times, however, when a single patch or regular surface generated from curves will not cut it. The problem comes when you get to a branching area, which is defined as something that can't be formed from a basic cylinder, sphere, or torus. The human torso is a good example of an object that has branches—the arms and legs create a topology that's impossible to completely cover with a single rectangular patch. If we use our gift-wrapping analogy, we would need more than one piece of paper and some tape to completely wrap a human body. If you don't believe this, get a hunk of wrapping paper and a Barbie doll or a GI Joe and try it yourself.

The way around this is to stitch the character together a patch at a time. This method can be painstaking, but it gives you the most control over the composition of a surface. The theory behind this method is very straightforward. Modeling starts with a single, four-sided patch created by deforming a single patch or generated from outline curves. A second patch is created, and its edge aligned with the edge of the first patch. A snapping function is then used to weld the vertices and edges exactly.

To join two patches, start with a single patch—in this case a Cardinal patch.

Bring in a second patch and roughly align three rows of vertices.

Use a snapping function to snap each row together. With three rows perfectly aligned, the patches will act as one.

It must be said that the edges themselves aren't technically welded together; they just occupy the same point in space. Because the vertices are in identical positions, however, they deform identically and appear to be welded together.

Some packages, such as 3D Studio MAX, streamline the process by enabling you to attach patch edges automatically. This saves you the tedium of snapping the patches together, a vertex at a time. Though tools like this are more efficient, the underlying theory is exactly the same. Other packages, such as Maya, have a number of tools to help maintain tangency between the surfaces, enabling seamless connections.

The best way to visualize a character made in this manner is to picture the patches as swatches of cloth. By "stitching" together the patches a vertex at a time, the patches are seamed together into a smooth and convincing character. You might want to study garment patterns as reference when using this technique.

In this case, the front and back of the torso, as well as an arm, are snapped together to create a seamless surface.

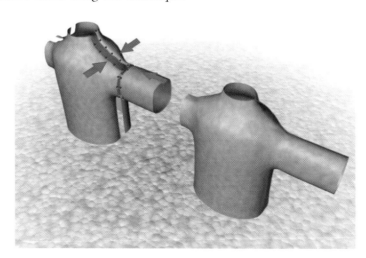

Three-Sided Patches

In most packages, patches are four-sided. This makes it easier to make the edges perfectly tangent. It also enables regular surfaces, which makes texturing much easier. Those modelers that support only four-sided patches, however, may have problems with objects that have branches, such as the arms and legs on a body.

Of course, any modeling package that can create a sphere from patches can arguably make a three-sided patch, because the top row of a sphere consists of triangles—or more specifically, four-sided patches that have one side collapsed to a point.

A three-sided surface is actually created as a bit of geometric sleight of hand. The surface created is geometrically a four-sided surface with the fourth side scaled to zero, making it look like a three-sided surface.

With that in mind, a four-sided patch can be made into a three-sided patch simply by snapping the points on one edge together so that they all occupy the same point in space. This essentially produces the same topology as the pole of a sphere, but in single-patch form. This works best on lower-order curves, such as cardinals, but also works with other patch types, including NURBS.

There are, however, a few packages that have support for three-sided patches out of the box, most notably in Discreet and Hash's products:

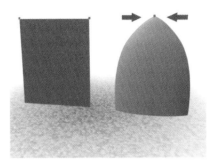

A three-sided patch is a four-sided patch with one side collapsed to a single point.

- Hash splines—Hash curves are a hybrid type of curve similar to cardinals but with the capability of interpolating endpoints. This means that Hash splines can define a surface with only three or four points. Hash also supports triangular patches. This enables you to create branching areas and nonregular topology, much like in a polygonal modeler. This keeps the character light while retaining the advantages of patches.

- MAX patches—Another unique type of patch are those found in 3D Studio MAX. These are closest to a Bézier-based patch, because each point has extra controls to manipulate the tangency of the surface, and the surface passes through the vertices. Like Hash, 3D Studio MAX also has the capability of creating triangular patches.

Modeling with NURBS

Tools that manipulate NURBS are very much like other types of spline modeling tools. Curves can be lathed or revolved to create surfaces such as spheres. NURBS curves can also be extruded or skinned to create patch- or tubular-shaped surfaces. Most NURBS modelers also support tools such as lofts, boundaries, and birails.

As has been stated before, one of the most difficult problems with patch surfaces, including NURBS surfaces, occurs in the branching areas. As with any other type of patch, NURBS surfaces can be seamed together by snapping the points together or by using special tools to help seam together the patches. These are shown in Table 2.2.

Curves on Surface

Another popular way to create branches with NURBS is by creating a curve on surface. This is done by locking a curve to the NURBS surface and then using these curves as the root attach points for the branches. There are two basic ways to get a curve on a NURBS surface:

- Draw the curve—The first is to draw the curve on the surface. In some of the more sophisticated packages, curves can be drawn in real-time directly on a NURBS surface. When drawn on the surface, a curve on surface will stay stuck to the surface no matter how the surface changes shape.

- Project the curve—The second way is to project an existing curve on a surface. Projected curves are simply curves that are projected onto a NURBS surface, much like a two-dimensional picture in a slide projector. Because the shape of the curve as it hits the surface is dependent on the angle of projection, you need to take this angle into consideration. Typically, the curve is projected at a right angle to the surface normals. When projected, a curve is locked to the surface; this means that if the surface changes shape, the curve will follow, exactly like a curve drawn on the surface.

One application for projected curves, and curves on surface in general, is to use them as the attach point for creating a second surface that remains seamlessly attached to the first. A projected curve, for example, can be used as the start of an extrude to create an arm or a tentacle.

Other Types of Curves on Surface

A trim curve is essentially a curve on surface. The trim curve gets its name from the fact that it is used to trim the surface away using the curve much like a cookie cutter. This enables you to punch holes in a NURBS surface, and is the closest you'll ever get to a NURBS Boolean operation. Trims are actually just a rendering trick. The entire surface still exists, and the portion trimmed away is not rendered.

A trim is a good base for creating branching surfaces. The trim avoids any problems with surfaces protruding through each other, because the potential protrusions have been snipped away by the trim operation.

Joining NURBS Surfaces

After you have a curve locked to a surface, you can use a number of methods for seamlesly creating additional branched surfaces. The theory of these tools follows the same logic: The curve on surface is used as a place to attach another surface. The trick lies in making this seam transparent to the eye.

Lofting to Curves on Surface

One method of making the seam transparent to the eye is to loft the curve attached to the surface along with other, unattached curves to create the skin. The base of the skin is locked to the originating curve, which, in turn, is locked to the original surface. One problem with this is that the skin hits the base surface at a right angle to the surface normals, creating a distinct seam.

To remedy this, some modelers use multiple curves on the surface as the base for the skin. Remember, that with NURBS curves, it takes four points to determine a curve. If three curves are locked to the surface, the surface should be perfectly tangent by the end of the third curve, eliminating the seam. Still, the texture might not line up exactly, so it is usually a good idea to feather the texture so it is transparent at the seam to get a nice smooth transition.

Blends

Another, more elegant solution of making the seam transparent is to use a NURBS blend. A blend differs from a skin, because it automatically creates enough surface to fill the area between two curves attached to a surface while maintaining perfect tangency. Because the blend is automatic and self-adjusting, it is a great choice for highly flexible areas, such as shoulders. Blends are also handy in facial areas. A nose or the area around the eyes can be blended into the surface of a face quite easily. The adaptive nature of the blend deftly sidesteps many of the detail and tangency problems inherent in a direct skin method.

One problem with blends concerns performance. A blend surface is very complex and can bog down a system during animation. In most packages, a blend shows up as a separate object, which means you can select and hide the blend objects while animating and then display them just before rendering.

Fillets

Other ways to create automatic surfaces is with tools that saw their genesis with CAD-type operations. The fillet is really just a variant of the blend that is constrained to a semicircular outline. It is great for creating rounded joints between attached surfaces.

Chamfer

The chamfer is the opposite of a fillet; it rounds the outside edge of a surface, rather than the intersection of two surfaces. The chamfer is perfect for rounding off the corners on a box, for instance.

Deformation by Surface

Deformation by surface is another tool that has been used by vendors such as Softimage to create seamless attach points. Instead of locking down a curve, deformation by surface locks an entire surface to another. This can be used to add local detail or to create a base to connect a branched surface, such as an arm or a leg. In Softimage, this is accomplished through the use of a Zip patch, which skins between a deformed patch and a free surface. One problem with deformation by surface is that the patches are not mathematically locked, so there is always a slight error in the fitting. Still, judicious use of textures can hide the seams.

Metaballs

Although these types of surfaces certainly are more than enough to create convincing characters, there are a number of other ways to create a 3D surface. The most common of these other methods used for characters is metaballs.

In their simplest form, metaballs are simply spheres or other primitive shapes that tend to blob together. Metaballs are a technology that 3D animators use to easily create round, blobby objects. As these objects move closer together, they seem to melt together.

In Other Words...

Metaball implementations cross a large range of packages, and the names may vary from package to package. Some packages allow metaballs modeling only, while others permit animation as well.

3D Studio MAX—Has no native metaballs, but several third party implementations are available.

Clay Studio Pro—Enables animation, muiltiple types of primitives, sticky mapping and spline driven muscles.

MetaReyes—Enables animation, sticky mapping, and the capability to create spline driven muscles.

Blob Modeler—A freeware modeler with no animation

Softimage—Meta Clay is Softimage's implementation and enables spherical and ellipsoidal objects as well as animation.

LightWave—Metaballs in LightWave enable spheres and are modeling tools only.

Houdini—Metaballs are spherical and ellipsoidal and enable animation.

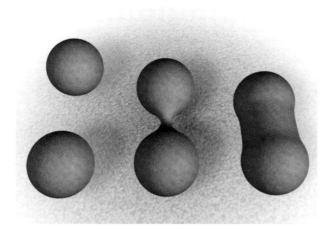

As metaballs get close, they blob together into a single object.

In addition to spheres, many of the better metaball implementations enable a variety of primitives, including cubes and spline-driven muscle shapes.

The "balls" in metaballs originally derived their name from simple spheres, which are the building blocks of metaball objects, though many of the better implementations enable a variety of primitives. By assigning each sphere a weight and a sphere of influence, the metaballs modeler fuses many spheres into a single blob. How much the spheres fuse really depends on the weights, influences, and distances between the spheres.

Here's a simple example. Consider two spheres of equal size. The sphere of influence surrounds each of the spheres like a shell. Any other sphere coming within this range tries to fuse with the spheres. The weight determines exactly how much fusion actually occurs. If we have two balls of equal size, they'll fuse at the intersection of their spheres of influence. The amount that they fuse depends on their weights. As weights and the spheres of influence change, you get different effects. A higher sphere of influence makes an object softer and more willing to fuse with another. On the other hand, if one sphere is given more weight than another, it appears more stable and solid.

Not all metaballs implementations are restricted to spheres. Many pack-ages allow nonspherical objects. Some go even further and actually enable you to create virtual muscles to give you some stunningly real effects.

The Trouble with Metaballs

The big problem with metaballs is that they create very messy surfaces that are difficult to animate, because most metaball modelers use the marching cubes algorithm to generate the surface. This means that a three-dimensional grid is projected over the model, and the software uses this to calculate where the surface exists. The artifact of this method is a model with a fine unidirectional mesh that completely covers the surface. This type of surface proves very difficult to animate in its raw form.

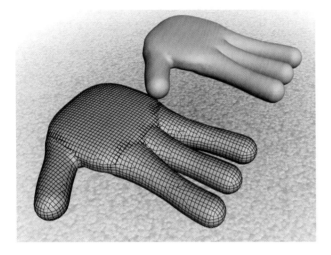

When a metaball-created model is turned into a mesh, the mesh may look smooth, but the underlying wireframe is usually a mess and impossible to animate.

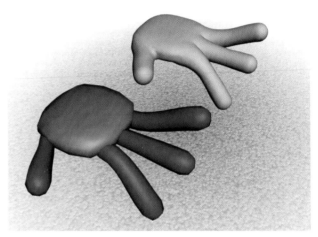

To solve this problem, the metaball primitives themselves are animated, and the mesh is resolved at render-time.

Animating Metaballs

There are two ways to circumvent the problem of metaball-derived meshes so you can animate the character. The first is to use the metaball-generated model as a template. The model is loaded into a more traditional modeling program, and the character is rebuilt using polygons, patches, or NURBS.

The second way to use metaballs in an animation environment is to animate the metaball primitives themselves and resolve the surface only at render-time. This gives you a great deal of flexibility and enables very soft and stretchy characters to be created. One good example is the motion picture *Flubber*, which used metaball technology for the jellylike characters that starred in the movie.

One issue with this form of animation comes into play when a texture is applied. The more sophisticated packages enable "sticky mapping," the capability of applying the texture to the metaball primitives themselves. This mapping then flows through to the surface and animates with the character. A less-sophisticated package may allow a texture to be applied only to the resulting surface, rather than the primitives. When animated, textures will not adhere to such a surface.

Conclusion

As you can see, there are many different types of surfaces that can be used to build a character. It is always a good idea to at least try all these surface types to determine what works best for you. Having experience in all the different geometry types will also make you more knowledge-able and valuable in the job market.

The next few chapters discuss modeling characters. The characters are built using a number of different geometry types. If your software allows it, take the time to work through all the exercises so that you under-stand how characters are built using a number of different techniques.

CHAPTER 3

Modeling Bodies for Animation

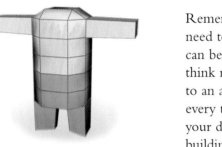

When you understand the basics of character design and the basics of modeling, you can begin building a character that's not only appealing, but animates well. The construction of your character is determined by its design and by your software's capabilities. Be sure to take advantage of your software's strengths when designing a character.

Remember that your characters not only need to look good, they also need to animate well. This means keeping your characters light so they can be easily manipulated. A character that moves as fast as you can think makes animation a breeze. There is nothing more frustrating to an animator than waiting a few seconds for a character to update every time it's moved. Fast interaction is accomplished by planning your detail so that there is no waste. Less is more when it comes to building characters.

The Structure of the Body

Whether you're designing a photorealistic human or a flour sack, you need to understand the basics of anatomy. Even a simple flour sack can appear to have feet and shoulders, so whether you're animating a flour sack to move like a human, or you're animating a CG human, knowledge of human anatomy is essential.

This chapter gives a brief overview of the basics of anatomy. The subject, however, is incredibly deep, and entire books have been written on the it. A good book on anatomy is always a great reference for modelers and animators alike. Another good place to get a strong foundation in anatomy is through a life drawing class. Visualizing the human form helps train the eye as well as aid the understanding of the human form.

The Skeleton

If you want to design humanlike characters that animate well, you need to understand the human skeleton—how it is put together and also how it moves. A human skeleton has over 200 separate bones. Many of these, however, are small bones, such as those found in the wrists, ankles, and inner ear. As an animator, you need to concern yourself with the major systems of the body and how those systems affect the shape and posture of the body as they move:

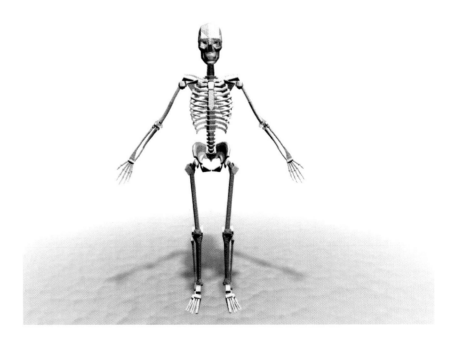

The Arms

Three major bones comprise the arm: the humerus, the radius, and the ulna. Proportionally, the arms hang down so the wrists are even with the hips.

The humerus is the upper arm. It is connected to the shoulder by a ball-and-socket joint. This gives the upper arm a wide range of motion.

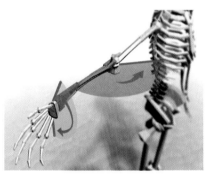

The forearm consists of two bones: the radius and the ulna. They are connected to the humerus at the elbow, which is a hinged joint, limiting the motion to one axis. The radius and ulna twist around one another to rotate the hand at the wrist.

The Shoulders

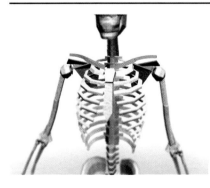

Two sets of bones comprise the shoulders. Along the front of the body is the clavicle, commonly known as the collarbone. Along the back is the scapula, a broad bone commonly known as the shoulder blade. Shoulders connect the arms to the spine, but also have a range of motion that enables them to "shrug" and to move forward and back slightly.

continues

continued

The Vertebrae

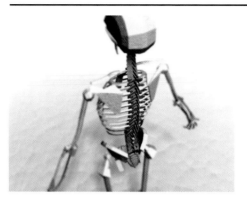

The vertebrae, better known as the spine, are the support system for the upper body. All the weight of the upper body is transmitted through the spine to the hips.

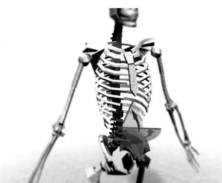

Alone, each vertebra bends only slightly, but as a system, the vertebrae enable the spine to twist and to bend at the waist.

The Hips

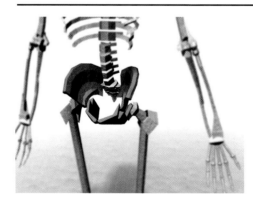

Several bones comprise the hips, most important of which is the pelvis. The hips anchor the spine and transfer the weight of the upper body to the legs. As such, they are the center of weight distribution for the entire body. The hips themselves don't move; the body moves in relation to the hips.

The Legs

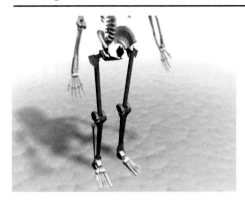

Like the arms, three bones comprise the legs. These are the femur, also known as the thigh bone, and the shin, which is two bones: the tibia and the fibula.

The femur attaches to the pelvis with a ball-and-socket joint. This gives the thigh a wide range of motion, though not quite as much as the shoulder gives the upper arm.

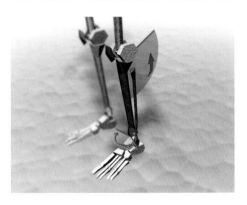

The shin is made up of the tibia and the fibula. They are connected to the femur at the knee, which is a hinged joint. The tibia and fibula also twist around one another to rotate the foot at the ankle.

Muscles

Bones define the structure of the body, and muscles, to a large degree, define the shape of the body. There are hundreds of muscles in the body, and each performs a specific function. Muscles do their work by contracting, or pulling, the bones and skin. In the body, there are a few major muscles that the modeler and animator need to understand:

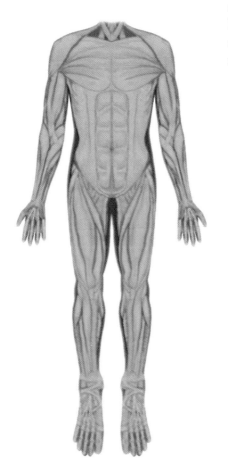

Deltoids—These are the muscles that run over the top of the shoulders and give the shoulders their definition. The deltoids raise the arm above the head.

Pectoralis/latissimus—The pectoralis major moves the arm down and forward. The latissimus moves the arm down and back.

Biceps/triceps—These are located around the humerus, or upper arm. The biceps pull the forearm up, and the triceps move it back.

Supinator—The supinator rotates the radius and ulna around each other, twisting the forearm.

Flexors/extensors—These are a few of the many muscles in the forearm and are the muscles that open and close the hand.

Gluteus maximus—The rear end, which enables the leg to move backward.

Sartorius/quadraceps—Also known as the biceps of the leg, the sartorius enables the shin to bend back at the knee. It is complemented by the quadraceps, which pulls the shin forward.

Gastrocnemius—This is the muscle along the back of the shin, and it is connected to the foot via the Achilles tendon.

Construction Methods

Most 3D packages offer a wide degree of choices when building a character. The geometry can be either polygonal, patch, or some other surface type, such as metaballs or membranes. The character can be built as one solid entity or broken up into its component parts.

Breaking up a character in parts is also known as segmenting a character. Depending on your character's design, it may be easier to segment the character rather than build it as one single skin. A good example of a segmented character might be an artist's mannequin or a suit of armor. Single-skinned characters, such as a seamless human, are typically more organic and lifelike.

Segmenting Bodies

Without a doubt, the easiest way to create a body is to create it as a series of segments. A true segmented character is constructed a joint at a time, each joint as an individual segment. To picture a true segmented character, think of a classic artist's mannequin, a character constructed from individual blocks of wood and fitted together with metal pins. Action toys, such as Hasbro's venerable GI Joe, are also good examples of segmented characters.

Modeling a segmented character is quite easy, because each joint is constructed separately. Modeling the joints individually makes them very easy to construct. Usually, the entire character is made of one type of geometry, but any combination of geometry types can be mixed if your software allows it. Because the individual joints of a fully segmented character don't change shape as the character is manipulated, this type of character is usually very easy to animate. Manipulation of the character is fast, because the computer does not have to calculate complex shape changes on-the-fly.

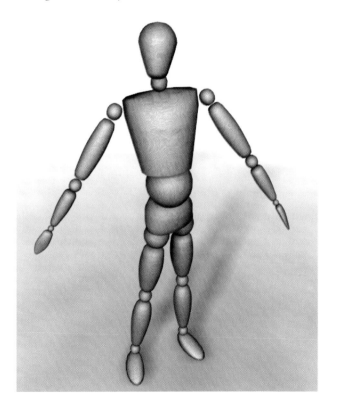

An artist's mannequin is a good example of a segmented character.

A robot is another good candidate for a segmented character.

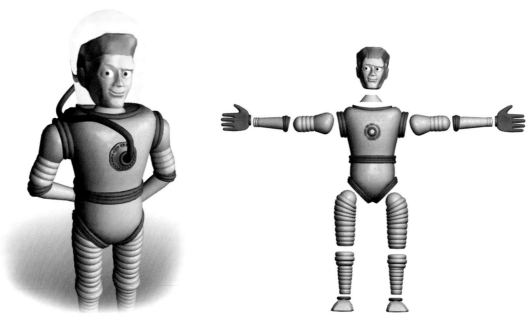

This space ranger's body looks seamless.

Pull him apart and you'll see that he is made of many different segments that have been cleverly hidden.

Clothing is a good device to hide seams. The seams for the hands on this character are cleverly hidden under the sleeves.

The downfall to segmentation is that, unlike a single-skin character, a segmented character will almost always have telltale seams. This may not be a problem if your character is designed to have seams—the artist's mannequin or a mechanical robot, for example.

Texture maps are very helpful in making a segmented character look real. A good, close-fitting seam covered with a complex texture will help hide, or at least minimize, the appearance of seams. Many popular interactive games use these methods to keep their characters looking good.

Another solution is to segment just the major chunks of a character. Many times, the head or the hands are created as separate objects that are connected to a seamless torso. The hands can be connected underneath a shirt sleeve, the feet connected underneath a pants leg, and the neck beneath a collar. Hiding the seam in such a manner still allows a realistic-looking character, but makes it easier to model and set up.

Characters can be segmented in many different ways. Here is a simple female character with obvious seams.

She is segmented in a number of places, but the hands and arms are seamless, as well as the feet and legs.

This character also has segments, but the seams are not as apparent.

Only the hands, head, and tail are separate. As you can see, there are many combinations when segmenting a character.

Modeling a Partially Segmented Body

Patches are another great way to create characters. In this exercise, you create a simple character that has a seam at the waist. The character is constructed of two simple spheres. This particular character was created using NURBS, but because there are no blended surfaces, it can be made in just about any package.

Exercise #1: Modeling a Simple Character with NURBS

1. Model the legs first. Start with a sphere.

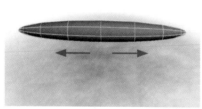

2. Rotate the sphere so that the poles lie along the horizontal axis. Scale the sphere along the horizontal axis to create a hot dog shape.

3. Select the vertices representing the ends of the hot dog and rotate them down to create a horseshoe shape.

4. Add detail near the hip area, and other places as needed, so that the legs can be sculpted.

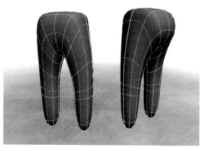

5. Sculpt the legs and hips to get the desired shape.

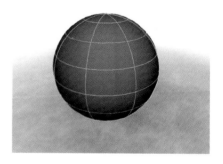

6. Put the legs aside for now while you build the upper body. Again, start with a sphere.

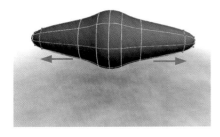

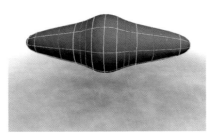

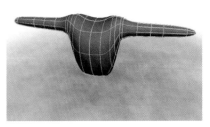

7. Rotate the sphere so that it lies along a horizontal axis. Select the vertices surrounding the poles and move them out to create arms.

8. Add detail near the armpits and along the chest so the arms and the upper body can be sculpted.

9. Resculpt the upper body to give it the desired shape.

10. Finally, join the two objects to create the body. This creates a seam where the two surfaces overlap. To hide this, a simple belt can be added around the waist to hide the seam. The hands, feet, and head can also be attached as segments.

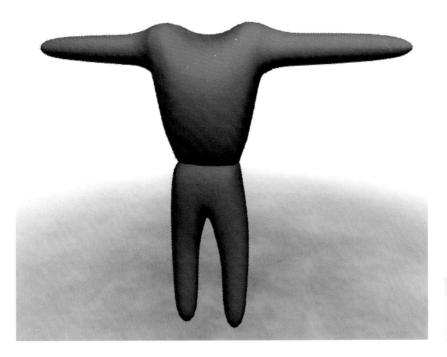

 On the CD

A copy of this model is on the CD. It is named SegGuy.

Seamless Characters

Although segmenting the parts of a body is one good way to build characters, many times you need the body to be one continuous skin. A more realistic or organic character, such as a realistic iguana, could not hide a seam between the head and body. In this case, you really need it to be all one piece, unless it's wearing a necktie. Many superhero characters wear tight-fitting garments, and can also be considered single-skin characters.

A single-skin character is certainly much trickier to construct than a segmented body. Still, the construction of such a character is certainly within the capabilities of most software. Both polygons and patches, as well as many other geometry types, can be used to create a seamless body.

A seamless body must be deformed in order for it to animate. Typically, the body is deformed using a skeletal deformation system. This, however, can be problematic if the body is not modeled properly. Usually, the problems arise in the areas with the widest range of motion. A quick look at our skeleton tells us that these spots are where the ball-and-socket joints are located–specifically, the shoulders and the hips. If the mesh is improperly constructed, you get an unnatural movement of the skin that may cause it to break or crease.

Proper modeling first means understanding anatomy and the way a body is put together. If your character's shoulder is anatomically incorrect, for example, it simply will not move properly. The shoulder is supposed to be above the armpit, for example. If the shoulder is modeled too far to the outside or inside of the armpit, not only will the character look odd, but the shoulder will not move properly when animated. It is always a good idea to place your detail only where it is needed and try to run that detail along the major lines of force exerted by the muscles.

Modeling a Seamless Body Using Polygons

Polygons can make excellent single-skin bodies. Because polygons give you wide topological freedom, the entire body can be modeled as a single surface, including the hands and the head. As with other polygonal modeling methods, it is best to model the hands at a low resolution and then add the required detail through subdividing the surface.

The body presented in the exercise creates a simple male figure without the head and hands, which are discussed in the next chapters. The modeling is done in two phases. First, the basic body is blocked out. Second, detail is added to the body where it is sculpted into the desired shape. When built, the model can be modified to create a body of just about any size and shape.

Exercise #2: Phase One—The Basic Body

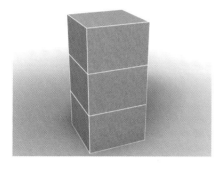

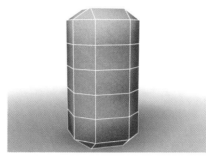

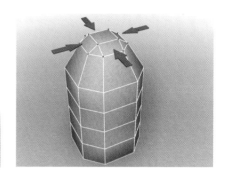

1. Start with a simple box that has three vertical subdivisions. The box should be of equal width and depth, with the height approximately three times the width.

2. Subdivide the box once. This should bevel the top, bottom, and sides, as well as add detail within the box.

3. Select the vertices defining the top two rows of edges. Scale these down equally to make a neck.

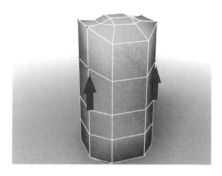

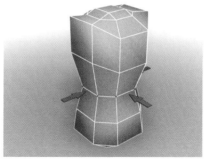

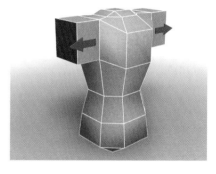

4. Select these vertices on the outer side of the body. Move these up vertically so that the shoulders are approximately even with the neck.

5. Select the vertices surrounding the waist and scale them in. (If you are making a heavyset character, you may want to scale these out instead.)

6. Select the faces at the base of the shoulders and extrude them out to create an arm stub.

continues

Exercise: continued

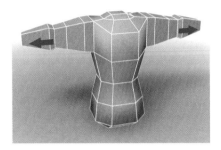  

7. Continue extruding the faces to create enough detail to define the rest of the arm. The faces can be scaled up or down to help define the outline of the arm. If you want, you can even extrude the hands from the ends of the arms.

8. Now move on to the legs. Select the outer faces on the underside of the body and extrude these down to create a leg stub.

9. Select the vertices defining the bottom face of the left leg stub. Scale these vertically to zero so that the face is horizontal. Do the same for the right leg.

 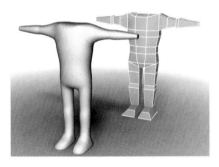

Note

Construction of hands is covered in the next chapter.

10. Now that they are horizontal, reselect the faces at the bottom of the leg stubs. Extrude these straight down to create the legs. As with the arms, add just enough detail to create the shape you want.

11. If all you want is a basic body, this model can be smoothed and used immediately (of course, hands and a head need to be added). To further refine the body, continue with the next phase.

Exercise #3: Phase Two—Adding More Detail

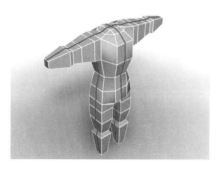

1. Before you refine the body, some extra detail needs to be added. Create an edge loop that bisects the front of the body and another that bisects the body along the side.

2. Add three more edge loops. One bisects the arms, running across the chest and along the back. The second two bisect each leg, running up and over the shoulders.

3. Select the vertices in the leg created by these new edge loops and scale them outward so that they give the leg a more cylindrical outline. Continue to refine the outline of the legs. Repeat this procedure for the arms.

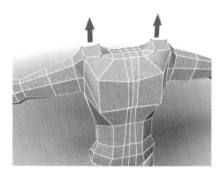

4. Refine the shape of the chest and shoulder area. Select the vertices that define the top of the shoulders. Move these up vertically to define the deltoids. Sculpt the chest area as well to define the pectoralis.

5. Select the faces in the top center of the body. Extrude these to create a neck stub. If you want, you can attach the head separately or continue extruding to create extra geometry, which can be fashioned into a head later (this will be discussed in Chapter 5, "Modeling Heads for Animation").

continues

Exercise: continued

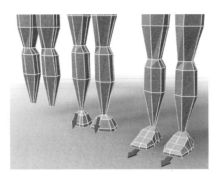
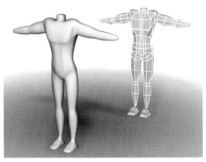

On the CD

A copy of this model is on the
CD. It is named PolyMan.

6. To make feet, extrude the
   faces at the bottom of the
   leg, and then scale them
   up to create the heel area.
   Select the forward faces and
   extrude them forward to
   create the rest of the foot.
   Hands can be made in a
   similar fashion, and detailed
   construction is discussed in
   the next chapter.

7. After the low-res model is
   complete, it can be subdivided and textured to make the
   high resolution final. If the
   body is being deformed by a
   skeletal deformation system,
   the subdivision should probably take place after the deformation takes place.

Modeling a Seamless NURBS Body

Most of the better NURBS implementations enable you to create a
blended surface. This exercise takes advantage of that feature to create a
seamless female body. Of course, the same techniques can be applied for
male, alien, or any other type of body you want to construct.

Exercise #4: Building a Seamless NURBS Body

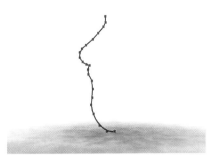

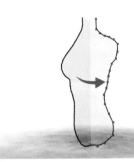

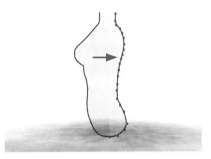

1. The torso is created using outline curves. First, create the profile of the front of the body. If you have sketches or a digitized model, use them as reference in creating this outline.

2. Duplicate this curve and rotate it 90 degrees. Select the vertices and reshape the curve to create the outline of the left side of the body. Again, reference may be helpful for this step. When completed, mirror this curve to create the right side of the body.

3. Duplicate the original curve and rotate it 180 degrees. Reshape the curve to create the back of the body. You should now have four curves representing the front, back, right, and left sides of the character.

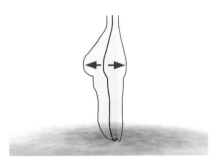

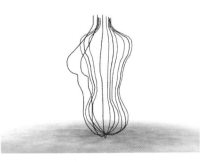

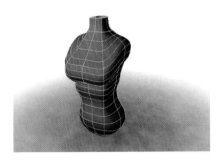

4. Select the front curve. Duplicate it and rotate the duplicate approximately 30 degrees to the right. Create a second duplicate for the left side.

5. Repeat this procedure for the other three curves. You will now have a total of 12 curves.

6. Loft or skin the curves to create a closed surface. If the outline curves were accurate, the torso will be close to the desired shape.

continues

Exercise: continued

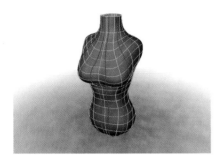

7. Insert detail as needed (red) and sculpt the torso to the final shape.

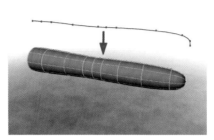

8. Put the torso aside while the arms are constructed. Create a hook-shaped curve and revolve it into an arm shape. (If you want to create an open-ended arm, such as a shirt sleeve, leave off the hook to get a cylinder open at both ends.)

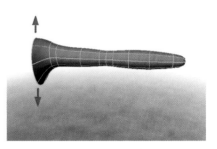

9. Sculpt the arm to get the desired shape. Select the inner side of the arm near the shoulder and expand it to create a funnel shape. Mirror the object to get the opposite arm.

10. Move the arm close to the torso. Extract the curve at the shoulder end of the arm. Project this curve onto the torso.

11. Trim out the surface within the projected curve.

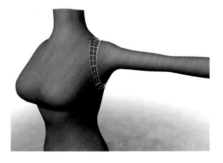

12. Create a blend between the trim curve and the end of the arm. Adjust the blend parameters to get a seamless fit. Repeat this procedure for the opposite arm.

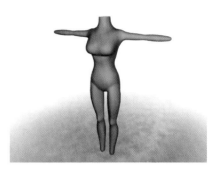

13. Create a leg the same way you created the arm. Revolve an outline curve, and then sculpt the resulting surface to create the desired leg shape. Mirror this leg to create the opposite leg.

14. Connect the legs to the body using a blend. This procedure is virtually identical to the arms. Curves are extracted from the legs and projected onto the torso. The surface is then trimmed, and a blend surface is created to fill the gap.

15. The completed body is ready for animation. Hands and feet can be created as separate objects or blended to the ends of the arms and legs. Because the body is open at the neck, a head can be attached seamlessly, separately, or through a blend.

Conclusion

The bodies outlined in the exercises have been very simple representations of realistic human bodies. Of course, one of the joys of animation is the capability to go far beyond reality. Any of the bodies can be reshaped and reworked into a character that suits your needs. Think of these bodies as basic building blocks. They are only the starting point for more witty, fantastic, or stylistic designs.

CHAPTER 4

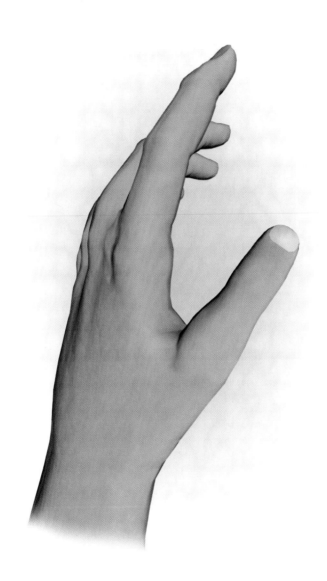

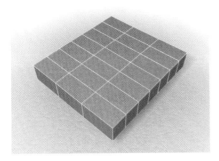

Modeling Hands for Animation

Next to faces, hands can be one of the more expressive parts of the human body. If you've ever watched anyone who gestures a lot, you know that hands can be a very important part of communication. In addition to helping with communication, hands also give humans the facility to manipulate and build things.

Animating hands can be particularly tricky. Like the person who's thrust upon a stage with no preparation, many animators don't know what to do with their hands—or, at least, the hands of their characters

The hand is a very complex structure, with dozens of bones, muscles, and tendons—all covered by pliable skin. Modeling the hand is a challenging task, and preparing it to be animated can prove frustrating as well. Like many complex tasks, however, modeling a hand can be broken down into simple steps that make the job easier.

Examining the Hand's Structure

Although hands are complex structures, they can be thought of as a collection of simple shapes. If you look at your own hand, you see that the palm is pretty much a rectangular box, with the fingers as cylinders attached along the top edge. The thumb is a stubbier cylinder attached at about a 45-degree angle in the bottom corner of the box. Depending on your character, you may need to create long, skinny hands, short, stubby hands, or something in between. Whatever the proportions, the basic shapes are essentially the same.

These basic shapes can simply be hierarchically linked, giving you a stylized, but serviceable, segmented hand. If you want a different look, you can expand and enhance these basic shapes with other, more sophisticated modeling tools. You can use almost any technology at your disposal. Polygonal hands are probably the easiest to model. Metaballs can also make hands, and a good NURBS modeler with blending capabilities can create excellent hands as well.

Another issue is how many fingers to use. A realistic character will have four fingers (and one thumb) on each hand. For some unexplained reason, many cartoon characters have only three fingers, and many alien characters only one or two. The fewer fingers a character has, the easier it is to build, but the techniques are the same, regardless.

The palm is basically rectangular, and the fingers are basically cylindrical.

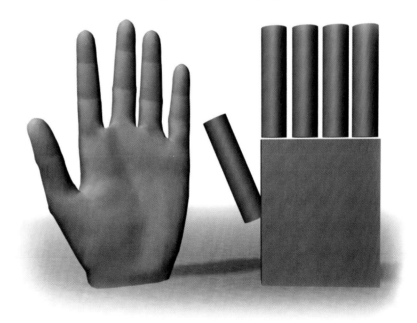

You can animate hands in a number of ways. If you build your hand out of segments, they can be joined in a hierarchy and manipulated directly. Hands built from metaballs also can be joined in the same manner as segmented hands and manipulated directly. Solid mesh or spline-based hands need to be animated with a mesh deformation tool that's controlled by a skeleton made of bones, which will be covered in a later chapter. You can also deform hands with shape animation tools, such as a multiple target morphing utility. Each method has its advantages and disadvantages, and which method you choose will depend on your character's requirements, as well as your software and its capabilities.

Flexibility of the Hand and Fingers

However you animate your character's hands, you should make sure that the hand is flexible enough to move realistically. How much the hand moves is, to some degree, an aesthetic decision. Some projects demand hands that look absolutely real, right down to the bulge of the knuckles and tendons. Other projects are less stringent and simply require that the fingers move well.

These decisions will affect how flexible your hand needs to be, as well as how it is built. A hand manipulated using a skeleton or shape animation will probably be more flexible than one made of hard segments, because the skin on the hand changes shape constantly as the hand flexes. It is a good idea to know ahead of time how much detail the art direction of your project requires for your character's hands.

Of course, the best way to see how a hand moves is to use your own as an example. Flex your hand and observe how it changes shape as it moves. Here are a few pointers to help you understand the hand and how it moves.

The Fingers

If you look at your own hand, the motion of the fingers is pretty obvious. Compare your own hand to the illustrations on the next page.

The last effect (the folding and creasing of the skin) is a tough one to create. Many projects don't require this level of detail, but you can achieve it with a skeleton and a mesh deformation utility that enables you to bulge and crimp the mesh according to the angle of the joint. Another way is to use a shape animation system that actually morphs the fingers to premodeled extreme shapes. There are also other deformation systems, such as spline or wire deformers, that can create the effect.

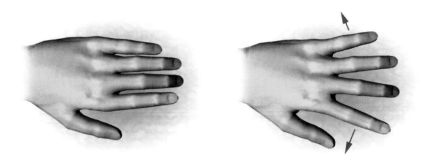

They angle out a bit when the hand spreads.

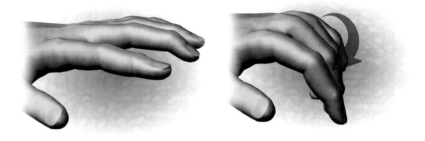

They can also curl toward the palm. When this happens, the pinky is usually the finger that curls first, with the other fingers following in order.

The skin creases and folds as the fingers bend (arrow).

The Thumb

The thumb's motion is a bit more complex than the other fingers. Its three joints give it a much higher degree of motion than the three joints of a finger. Again, look at your own thumb and notice how it compares to the following illustrations.

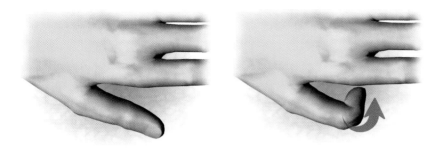

The top joint of the thumb bends toward the palm.

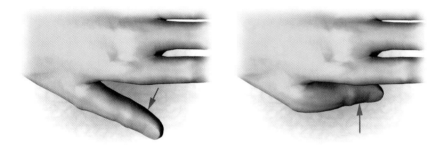

The second joint pulls the entire thumb toward and away from the palm.

There is actually a third joint in the thumb, forming the base of the palm, hidden inside the skin. This joint enables the thumb to move below the plane of the hand.

This last type of motion also causes the skin in the palm to crease. Again, most hands don't need this level of detail. A skeletal deformation system can be used to manipulate the skin, and a multiple target morphing system or other type of deformer is required for you to animate the crease.

This flexibility enables the thumb to reach over and touch all the fingers. This one bone is what gives humans their "opposable thumbs," which separates them from the rest of the animal kingdom.

Modeling Methods for Hands

As with bodies, you can model hands out of segments, metaballs, polygons or patches, or any other type of surface, depending on your software. Most modeling methods can produce hands that look good and move realistically.

In these exercises, construction of hands from a number of different methods will be discussed. Hopefully, one of these will work for you. Also, in each exercise, only one hand is modeled. It is simply a matter of mirroring your newly created hand to make its counterpart.

Modeling Segmented Hands

Segmented hands are very easy to construct and, although they may not be seamless, they still can be quite expressive. Characters such as insects, robots, and low-resolution characters for interactive use all are places where a segmented hand can be used. The characters in Pixar's *A Bug's Life* are a terrific example of segmented hands.

Exercise #1: Building Segmented Hands

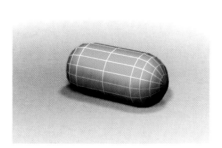 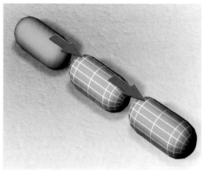 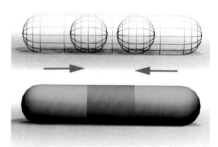

1. Start with a simple finger joint. This particular joint has two hemispheres at the ends.

2. Copy the finger joint to create two more joints.

3. Align the fingers together. Because the original joint was made out of a hemisphere, you can align the joints in wireframe so that the hemispheres line up. This will make the joint almost seamless when it animates.

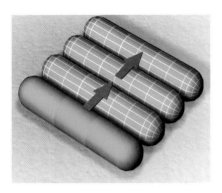 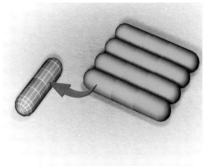 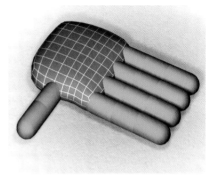

4. Copy the finger to create more fingers.

5. Copy two joints of a finger to make a thumb.

6. Model a palm, and then link the hierarchy.

Compared to a seamless hand that needs to be deformed, a segmented hand is also easy to set up. Segmented hands also can be animated quite easily. They are great for practicing your animation chops.

This, of course, is a very basic, but useful hand. The big point here is that the hand is a collection of objects that are linked in a hierarchy. For more complex creatures, the individual shapes can be molded to whatever shape your character demands.

Modeling Hands from Polygons

Because polygons offer a wide degree of topological latitude, they make an excellent choice for modeling hands. As with other polygonal modeling methods, it is best to model the hands at a low resolution and then add the required detail through subdividing the surface.

The hand presented in the exercise will block out the basic topology of a four-fingered hand. The techniques can easily be modified to produce just about any type of hand.

Exercise #2: Building Hands from Polygons

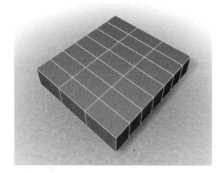

1. Start with a simple box that has 8 rows of vertices in the X direction, 4 rows in the Y direction and 2 in the Z direction.

2. Select the highlighted edges and move them toward the center of the hand. The spacing between these edges and their neighbors will eventually determine the spacing between the fingers.

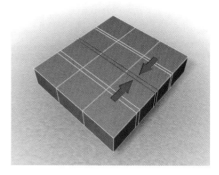

3. Do the same with the inner edges. Move them together so they reside in the center of the hand and are about the same distance apart as the other two sets of edges.

4. Select the face along the front part of the box that represents the pinky and extrude it slightly to create a finger stub. The extrude should be the length of the first finger joint.

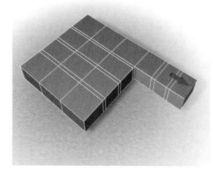

5. Extrude the same face again to make a narrow segment that defines the joint between the two joints. This will help the finger bend when it is deformed. Next, extrude the face again to make the middle joint. Repeat this process once more for the last joint.

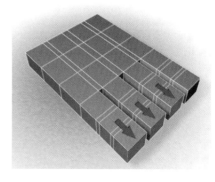

6. Repeat this process for the other fingers.

7. Now for the thumb. Select the face that resides at the bottom corner of the palm, diagonally from the pinky. Extrude this face slightly.

8. Extrude it again to make the first thumb joint, then a small gap between the joints, and finally the last joint.

9. Select the faces representing the thumb and rotate them along the vertical axis 45 degrees toward the palm.

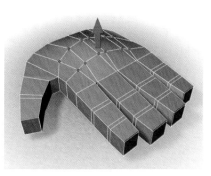

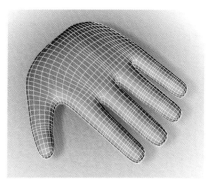

10. The basic topology is now in place. Start sculpting the hand to get the proportions correct.

11. When sculpting the hand, be sure to model the arch of the back of the hand, as well as the palm. To get the arch, select the vertices over the center of the hand and pull them up. You should also turn the hand over to sculpt the base of the palm in a similar manner.

12. When the hand is the correct shape, you can subdivide the surface to get a more detailed and smoother hand. If the hand is being deformed by a skeletal deformation system, however, this subdivision should take place after the deformation.

When the hand is done, it can be attached to the ends of your character's arms. If you want a totally seamless character, the basic box used as the starting point for the hand can be extruded from the character's arm. The hand can also be attached by building faces from the end of the arm to the base of the hand. This capability is one of the big advantages of polygonal modeling.

Of course, this hand is very basic. As you will see later, more detail can be added for an even more realistic look. And for a more stylized look, the hand can also be modified however you see fit.

Modeling a Hand with NURBS

NURBS can be used to model fairly realistic hands, though the methods required are a little more complex than with polygonal modeling. Because NURBS surfaces are regular surfaces, the branching areas where the fingers attach represent the big problem. This makes NURBS hands a bit more difficult to manage at animation time.

This exercise solves this problem using a NURBS blend to attach the fingers to the hand. The thumb and wrist can also be attached using a blend, but proper planning can eliminate a blend at these joints. The thumb has the largest range of motion, so try to avoid a blend in this area because of the tendency for blends to break and crack.

There are many ways to create a hand using NURBS; the choice will be dependent on the amount of detail required, the range of motion required, and the physical look of the character. The following sections describe two basic methods that can be expanded upon as you need.

Modeling a Hand with a Seamless Wrist

Here is a simple four-fingered hand that has a seamless thumb. The hand is also arranged so that it is open at the wrist, enabling a seamless attachment to the forearm at the wrist. This reduces the number of blends to four (one for each finger), which makes the hand easier to texture and deform.

Exercise #3: Building a Hand and Seamless Wrist

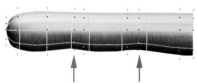

1. Start by making a finger. The finger is constructed by modeling a simple hook-shaped curve.

2. The curve is then revolved 360 degrees to make an open-ended sausage shape.

3. This open sausage shape can then be sculpted a bit more to give it a more realistic outline.

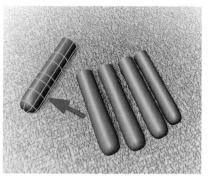

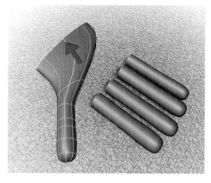

4. After the finger is modeled, copy it to make the other three fingers. Fingers are usually not the same size, so resculpt the new fingers accordingly.

5. Copy the original finger once more. Rotate the copy 45 degrees and place it roughly where the thumb resides.

6. We now need to make the surface of the hand. Select the vertices at the base of the thumb. Rotate them 45 degrees, and then scale them up to approximate the wrist opening.

continues

Exercise: continued

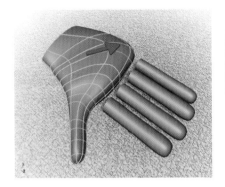

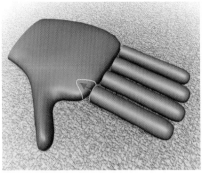

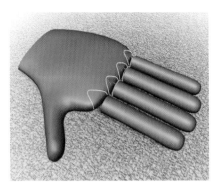

7. Now sculpt the rest of the hand from the base of the thumb. To get the shape right, you need to insert detail by adding rows of vertices into the hand. Add the detail gradually, so that you don't introduce unwanted creases into the hand.

8. When the hand is properly sculpted, the fingers need to be attached. Extract a curve from the base of the first finger, and then scale it up by about 10 percent. Project this curve onto the hand.

9. Do the same for the rest of the fingers. Make sure the projected curves do not overlap each other. If this happens, reposition the fingers and try again.

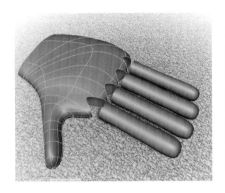

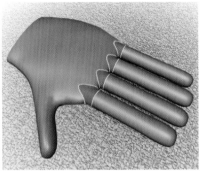

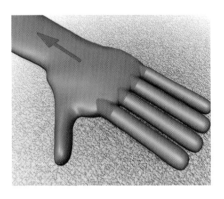

10. Use a trim operation to remove the surface of the hand within the boundaries of the projected curves.

11. Blend between the base of the fingers and the edges of the trims. The hand is now complete.

12. Because the base of the hand is open, the hand can be extended seamlessly from the wrist to create an arm. Conversely, an existing arm could have been resculpted to create the palm and thumb.

Modeling a NURBS Hand with a Blended Wrist

This next hand is very similar to the previous hand, but with a slight change in topology. This enables the detail in the hand to run parallel to the fingers, which makes it easier to construct details, such as knuckles and tendons. The big disadvantage is that the new topology forces you to add a fifth blend where the hand meets the wrist.

Exercise #4: Building a Hand and a Blended Wrist

1. The fingers and thumb are modeled the same as in the previous exercise.

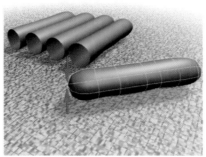

2. Close up the end of the thumb by scaling the end row of vertices to zero. This will make the thumb a closed sausage shape.

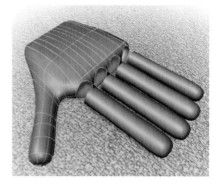

3. Move the vertices representing the base of the thumb so that it rests immediately below the pinky. Rotate these vertices 45 degrees.

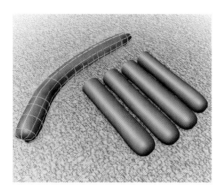

4. Add detail into the thumb. You should add at least two rows of vertices for every finger, plus a few more.

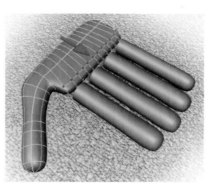

5. Select the vertices along the front side of the thumb and pull them forward to make the front part of the hand.

continues

Exercise: continued

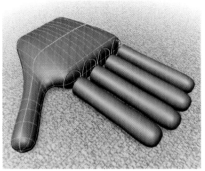

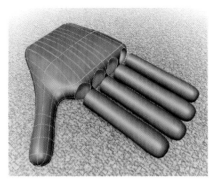

6. Select the vertices along the back side of the palm and move them back toward the wrist. The hand is now taking shape. Sculpt it to get the proper shape, adding detail if needed. Because the detail in this hand runs parallel to the fingers, it should be easy to create knuckles and tendons.

7. When the hand is sculpted to your satisfaction, attach the fingers as in the previous exercise. First, project curves extracted from the fingers onto the hand.

8. Use a trim operation to remove the surface of the hand within the boundaries of the projected curves.

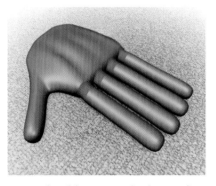

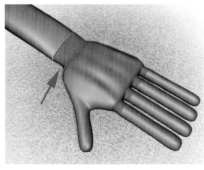

9. Blend between the base of the fingers and the edges of the trims. The hand is pretty much complete.

10. Because the detail runs parallel to the fingers, the hand and the arm can't be part of the same surface. To attach the hand to the arm, trim away the base of the hand and create a fifth blend surface in the same manner as you did for the fingers.

Modeling Metaballs Hands

Metaballs are another way to make a smoothly skinned hand. The modeling techniques for a metaballs-based hand are very straightforward, and the basic hand is very similar to a segmented hand. In this exercise, we will be using metaballs primitives, such as ellipsoids, which may not be supported by all the software on the market. For those who are limited to spheres, it is quite easy to fashion an ellipsoid out of a few spheres. This hand is very basic, and a more complex hand will require more primitives. One downfall to a metaballs hand is that it can be harder to sculpt realistic details, such as tendons and knuckles, using basic primitives such as ellipsoids.

Exercise #5: Building Smooth Hands with Metaballs

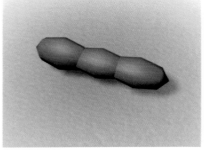

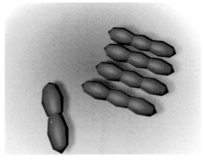

1. Start with a simple ellipsoid shape. This will become a finger joint.

2. Duplicate this shape three times. Move the shapes to create a primitive finger.

3. Duplicate the one finger to create the rest of the fingers. Copy two joints to create the thumb. Position these in the appropriate place.

4. Create a shape for the palm. In this case, a squashed ellipsoid is used, but you could certainly use more primitives to create a more complex shape for the palm.

continues

Exercise: continued

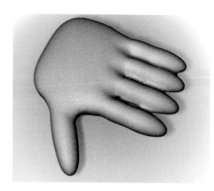

5. When these shapes are in place, the hand should start to blob together. Most likely, the fingers will tend to overlap, causing a webbing effect.

6. To get rid of the unwanted blobbing, create individual groups for each finger and the thumb. Each group will contain only those joints associated with the finger, along with the objects for the palm.

7. Animating the metaball primitives animates the hand, keeping it seamless.

This basic metaballs hand shows you yet another way to create a hand. As with the others, the hands are basic building blocks that can be expanded upon to create more complex or stylized hands. Regardless of the shape or the look of the hand, however, the building blocks are the same.

Adding Realism

As you can see, the hand is a very complex object to construct. All these exercises created simple hands that will work quite well for simple characters. The more realistic a hand gets, however, the more attention to detail is required. A totally real hand will have fingernails, skin that creases and folds, and knuckles and tendons that show themselves as the fingers bend.

For totally realistic hands, it is probably best to construct the hand out of polygons or patches. Because segmented hands, by definition, don't have a flexible skin, organic realism is nearly impossible. Metaballs-based hands can theoretically get quite realistic, but the tricks and techniques required are usually very software-specific, and outside the scope of this book.

Fingernails

Fingernails are probably the first detail that needs attention. A fingernail can be created in one of two ways. First, the nail can be modeled as part of the finger itself. For short nails this is fine. In fact, a simple indentation where the nail resides, combined with a good texture map of a fingernail might provide enough detail, particularly if the hands are never seen up close.

Claws and talons can also be made as an integrated part of the finger. Because claws tend to be cylindrical or conical in shape, they can be thought of as an extension of the cylindrical finger.

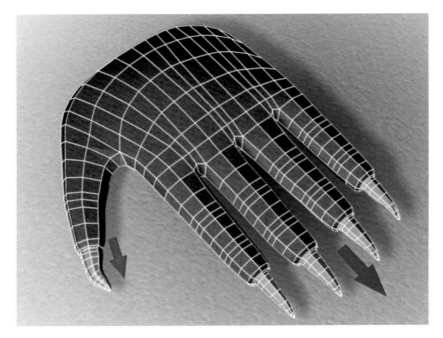

Because claws tend to be cylindrical or conical in shape, they can be thought of as an extension of the cylindrical finger.

The second way of doing nails is to make separate fingernail objects and attach them to the ends of the fingers, much like fake fingernails in real life. This is probably better for characters with longer fingernails, and can work quite well for creatures who sport claws and talons.

Knuckles

Along with fingernails, knuckles tend to be a good place to add detail to the hand. Knuckles that bulge out as the fingers curl in will add a sense of realism that will go a long way in selling the hand. Modeling knuckles is not much of a problem. Getting them to bulge correctly, however, requires a sophisticated deformation system.

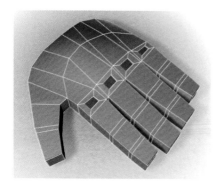

On a polygonal hand, a knuckle can be made quite simply by faceting the faces along the top of the hand that lie at the base of each finger.

Modeling a knuckle is fairly straightforward. You merely add enough detail in the area of the knuckle and sculpt it. On the polygonal hand we built, a knuckle can be made quite simply by faceting the faces along the top of the hand that lie at the base of each finger. On a NURBS-based hand, use the blended wrist model, which has the splines oriented in the proper direction. This should enable you to sculpt the detail properly.

Tendons

Tendons extend out from the knuckles and disappear under the skin somewhere before the wrist. Tendons can be made in much the same way as knuckles; all that is needed is enough detail to get the effect of a rising tendon.

On a polygonal hand, you will already have a line of edges running along the top of the hand toward the wrist. These edges can be faceted to create the additional detail needed. On a NURBS-based hand, it is again best to use the blended wrist model, which has the splines oriented in the proper direction to sculpt the tendons.

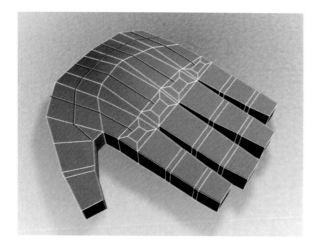

Adding extra detail along the back of the hand enables you to model tendons.

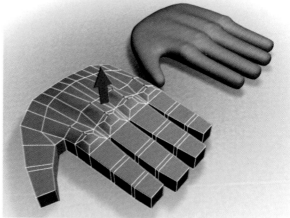

Move the vertices in the extra detail up; this helps create tendons. More detail can be added, if needed.

Skin Creasing

If you've had your palm read, you know that the hand is full of creases and lines. Not only do creases run along the palm, but also along the top of the knuckles, at the wrist, and a number of other places.

As with modeling elsewhere on the body, modeling with wrinkles and creases in mind can help when you need to add such detail. For example, if the detail of the hand is running along the same lines as the crease, the hand may just naturally crease as it moves. If not, you need to model more detail and force a crease.

Another efficient method is to create a bump or displacement map that can be animated as the hand moves. If you want to create actual geometry for the creases, your best bet is to choose a polygonal surface, because it enables this sort of detail to be sculpted in very specifically.

Webbing

The last consideration is the slight amount of webbing between the fingers. This occurs between all the fingers, but is most pronounced between the thumb and forefinger. This can be sculpted in quite easily on a polygonal model via a series of edges.

On a NURBS model, the blends at the fingers create an area that cannot be sculpted, which makes webbing between the fingers a bit difficult. Webbing between the fingers is not nearly as noticeable as the webbed region between the thumb and forefinger, however. In the hands created in this chapter, the thumbs are not blended, which enables the webbing effect to be sculpted as needed.

On many characters, this effect is small enough to be negligible; but on some types of characters, such as older people, for example, the effect is more pronounced. If the webbing is incredibly pronounced, such as a duck or the Creature from the Black Lagoon, the webbing may have to be built as a separate surface.

Conclusion

As you can see, there are many ways to build a hand that can be animated. It is always a good idea to try a number of different techniques and become fluent with them all. Also remember that you can mix and match geometry types. You may find that a metaballs-based hand works best for your NURBS-based character. In any event, be sure to keep your options open when approaching your characters.

CHAPTER 5

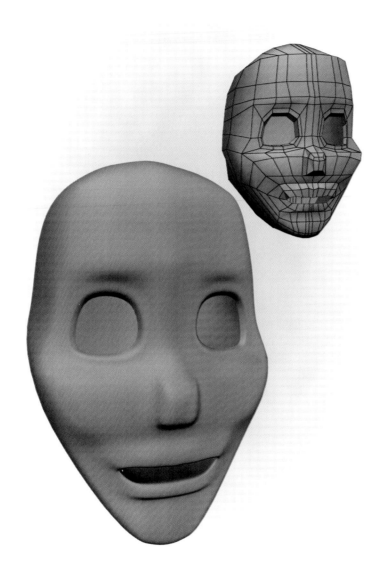

Modeling Heads for Animation

Modeling Heads for Animation

The head and face are very complex structures that are not easy to model, let alone animate. Sculptors spend years learning how to create convincing heads and faces, and modeling a convincing head on the computer takes just as much practice. Adding to this task is the need for your digital faces to also be animated easily. Modeling a face is one thing; modeling one that animates well is another. The human face can express a wide variety of emotions through the subtlest changes in shape.

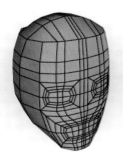

Don't despair, however. The goal of creating a totally convincing face in the computer is something that eludes even the best animators. The basic methods used to construct faces are pretty much the same, regardless of how real or stylized the face may be. After you've blocked out a basic head, it can be modified and shaped into almost any type of character. With a few of these tricks up your sleeve, you'll construct heads and faces that work quite well.

The Structure of the Head and Face

In order to build digital heads and faces, you need to understand the underlying anatomy of the human head and face. The face is by far the most important part of the equation, because this is where the majority of the movement takes place. The head typically acts as a solid frame for the face to live in. Outside the facial area, the rest of the head doesn't move much.

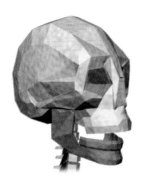

The head consists of two large masses: the skull and the jaw.

The head is basically made from two large bones: the skull and the jaw. The skull is really a collection of many smaller bones that are stitched together by cartilage. It can be thought of as a single mass balanced on the top of the spine. The jaw is the second major bone. Its movement affects the shape of the lower part of the face. When the mouth opens wide, it is the jaw's rotation that does all the work. Although we don't see the skull and jaw, their influence affects the structure and movement of the face and the muscles that cover it.

The Muscles of the Face

The face is a complex collection of muscles that pull and stretch the skin in a variety of ways. Understanding how these muscles work will guide you in the construction of your character's head and face. Let's take a look at these muscle groups.

a. Levator labii superioris—This muscle starts at the base of the nose and connects to the middle of the top lip. Used alone, it pulls the top lip up into a sneer.

b. Zygomatic major—This muscle lays across the cheek and connects to the corner of the mouth. Used alone, it pulls the mouth into a smile.

c. Risorius—This muscle stretches over the jaw and attaches at the corner of the mouth. Used alone, it pulls the mouth to the side and down, as when crying.

d. Triangularis—This muscle stretches over the lower side of the jaw and pulls the corner of the mouth down. It is used when frowning or scowling.

e. Depressor labii inferioris—This muscle connects the lower lip to the chin. It pulls the lower lip straight down, as when speaking.

f. Mentalis—This muscle connects to the skin of the chin. When contracted, it pulls the chin up, forcing the lower lip into a pout.

g. Orbicularis oris—This muscle is attached to the corners of the mouth. It purses or tightens the lips.

h. Orbicularis oculi—This muscle connects the cheek to the inner-eye area. Contraction of this muscle results in squinting.

i. Levator palpebrae—This muscle attaches to the upper eyelid and raises it when surprised.

j. Corrugator—This muscle runs from the bridge of the nose to the middle of the eyebrow. It pulls the eyebrows down and in, as when frowning or concerned.

k. Frontalis—This muscle runs across the forehead and connects to the eyebrows. It pulls the eyebrows up.

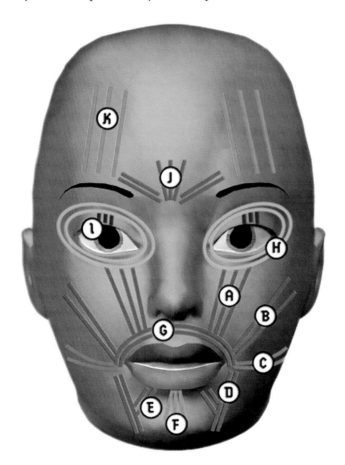

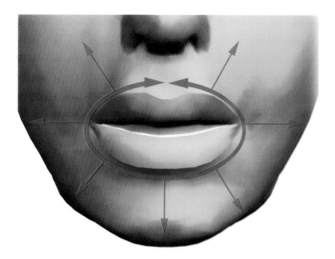

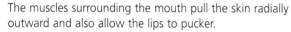

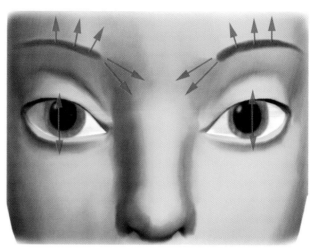

The muscles surrounding the mouth pull the skin radially outward and also allow the lips to pucker.

The muscles around the eyes move the brows up and down, as well as open and close the eyelids.

All this anatomy is great, but how does it affect the way a digital model is created and animated? The trick is to understand how these muscles pull and shape the face to create expressions. Really, the groups of muscles fall into two categories: lower face muscles that control the mouth and jaw, and upper face muscles that control the eyes and brows.

At the mouth, the muscles do three major types of movements. First, the muscles that lie across the cheeks and jaw pull the lips outward radially from eight major anchor points. Second, the muscles surrounding the lips contract to purse the lips, forcing them together and forward. Finally, the jaw can drop.

At the eyes, the muscles make three major movements. First, they open and close the eyelids. Second, the frontalis muscles on the brow raise and lower the eyebrows. Third, the corrugator pulls the eyebrows in toward the bridge of the nose, furrowing the brow.

If we can create a digital model that moves easily along the same lines that these muscles are pulling, we have a much better chance at animating the face convincingly.

Basic Head Modeling Methods

When designing a digital head, it's best to take a good inventory of your animation tools before starting. It is very easy to back yourself into a corner by designing a head that cannot be easily animated. There are a plethora of ways to create and animate a face, so it is up to your imagination and creativity to think up new and innovative ways to get this task done.

Paste-On Features

Using paste-on features is probably the easiest way to model and is one that has many of its roots in clay and puppet animation. Think of Gumby or Mr. Potato Head. These characters had a simple shape for the head with the features simply tacked on. The Rankin-Bass Christmas specials of the '60s (*Rudolph the Red-Nosed Reindeer, Santa Claus Is Coming to Town*) used this method effectively with puppets, and the same principles apply to digital animation as well.

With paste-on features, most or all of the character's features are separate objects. This frees the animator from complex modeling and shape animation.

The paste-on features can be made with the simplest of objects. Eyes can be simple spheres, the mouth is easily constructed from a torus, and the nose is a simple sphere. Replacement animation methods can also be used for the mouth. Animating shapes as simple as these is easy in most packages.

This character has a simple face.

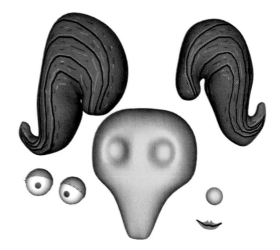

As you can see, most of the facial features, including the nose, are pasted on.

This is another character with paste-on features.

The mouth on this character is built in, but the rest of the features are separate objects.

This face is a simple texture map, but it still maintains a lot of character.

Another method you can use is to paint the features on with animated texture maps. This makes the modeling task downright easy, because the head can be as simple as a sphere—the detail is in the maps. They are drawn and animated by hand or in a 2D paint/animation package. This technique can prove cumbersome, however, because matching up the 2D animation of the face to the 3D animation of the body usually requires flipping between several packages. This sort of animation is best left to techniques such as replacement animation; the transparency of the texture maps or the visibility of the geometry containing the texture maps is animated to make the mouths appear and disappear.

A Face with Flexible Skin

For realistic and quasirealistic faces, you construct a head and face with skin that moves and flexes. This requires more complex modeling methods. It also requires a package that can support sophisticated shape animation of the many different expressions and poses the head and face will take.

Polygonal Heads

Polygons can make faces that are very realistic. The advantage to constructing a face with polygons is that you have much more control in defining the surface of the face. It is much easier to cut holes for eye sockets and nasal passages with polygonal methods.

To get a smooth head with polygonal methods, however, you need to have a lot of detail. Performing the complex shape animation required to deform such a head can tax even the fastest system. To circumvent this problem, a low-resolution version of the head can be animated and the detail added through subdivision after the deformation takes place. If this is not possible, a matching high-resolution version of the head can be swapped at render-time. With care and attention to detail, however, it is possible to animate faces quite effectively with a good polygonal animation package.

Patch-Based Heads

Patch-based heads are another terrific way to create digital flesh. Modeling a head with patches enables you to create faces that closely simulate the real thing. Because patches define a smooth surface with a smaller number of vertices than polygonal methods, controlling the shape of the face and maintaining a smooth surface is quite easy.

Modeling with patches is an exercise in Bauhausian simplicity. Less is more, and form follows function. Keeping your models light is the key. The simpler the structure of your digital head, the easier it will be to animate. Every time you add a control point, vertex, or extra spline, consider exactly what its function will be. If you don't need it, don't put it in your model. The lighter and simpler your models, the better.

Many patch modelers can restrict you to surfaces without holes or breaks. To get around this limitation, you need a NURBS-based modeler with trims, which enable you to punch holes in the surface. Without trims, eye sockets and mouth holes can be somewhat difficult to model. Whatever your particular modeler's capabilities, patch-based heads can be constructed using a number of different methods and topologies.

Topology and Facial Modeling

When modeling a face, you need to consider the way the face moves. Careful study of the muscle chart in the first part of this chapter shows that the muscles around the mouth pull the lips radially outward, but the brows are more horizontally oriented. This knowledge can guide you in the construction of your face.

You also need to consider the design of your character. A realistic human has different requirements than a stylized character—a cartoon dog with a long snout, for example. If your character needs the head to be seamlessly attached to the body, you may also need to consider different methods. Many times, the best solution is a compromise; the head may not be ideally constructed, but it makes the rest of the body easy to manage.

Topologically, a head can be thought of as a deformed sphere. The sphere can be oriented any one of three ways: with the "north pole" of the head at the top of the head, at the front of the head (mouth), or at the side of the head (ears). The orientation of the sphere when you start modeling affects how the final model will look when animated.

The following methods apply primarily to patch- and NURBS-based heads, but the techniques can also be applied to polygonal models. Of course, polygonal modelers have a bit more freedom with the topologies that they can manage.

The Pole at the Top of the Head

The pole at the top of the head is the topology that usually comes first to mind for most modelers, and many good-looking heads have been built this way. This method has two main advantages. First, the pole at the bottom can be opened up, allowing the character to seamlessly connect to the torso. This is important for NURBS modelers who want to limit the number of blends in a body. Second, the detail in the head runs horizontally, which enables better control of the eyes and brows.

The big disadvantage concerns the area around the mouth. Horizontal lines work great for the eyes, but not for the mouth. To get a decent mouth cavity, a number of splines must be bunched up at the corners of the mouth. This can cause creases that show up when the mouth is animated. If your character doesn't talk, however, this may not be a concern.

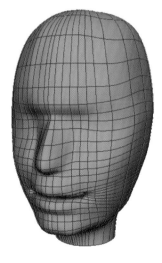

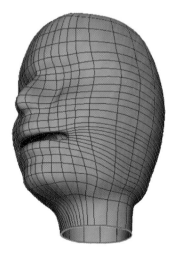

With the pole at the top of the head, the detail is arranged horizontally.

This topology also enables an open neck, which makes for a seamless attachment to the torso.

The Pole at the Mouth

Also known as a radial head, the pole at the mouth method is very effective and certainly makes the best mouths. By placing the pole at the mouth, the detail naturally flows along the same radial lines as the muscles of the face. This topology makes animation of the mouth quite smooth and easy. The radial method may limit you when it comes to modeling internal eye sockets, however, because the orientation of the splines can be off.

This can be overcome by sweeping the detail of the sphere up toward the top of the head. This enables you to sculpt the detail so that it is nearly horizontal at the brows, giving you the capability to sculpt the eyes more effectively.

Sweeping the detail up in this manner, however, causes another limitation where the head connects to the neck. The head will need a seam for the neck. Many times, this is not a problem. If the neck needs to be seamless, however, the detail must be swept down rather than up, and the detail around the eyes sacrificed. Deciding which is more important depends on the design of your character. A character with separate eyes and eyebrows, for example, will not need detail at the brows, allowing for a seamless neck.

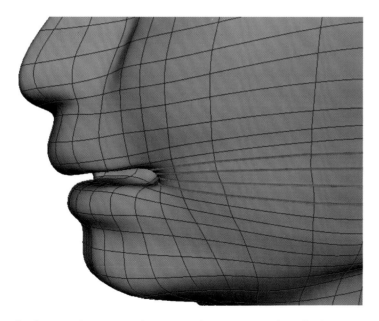

The disadvantage is, to get a decent mouth cavity, a number of splines must be bunched up at the corners of the mouth, which can hamper animation.

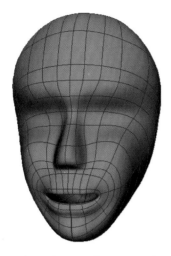

Putting the pole at the mouth creates a head that has a very flexible mouth.

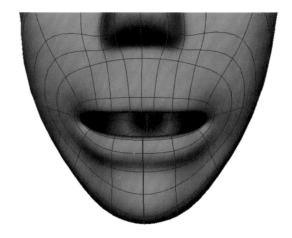

A closer view of the mouth shows the radial mouth, where the splines are arrayed radially, just like the muscles that surround the mouth.

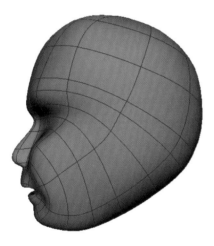

Sweeping the detail of the head toward the top makes the brows and eyes easier to model, but forces you to place a seam at the neck.

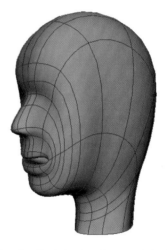

Sweeping the detail of the head toward the bottom makes the brows and eyes harder to model, but gives you an open neck, which enables a seamless attachment to the torso.

The Pole at the Ears

The pole at the ears is the least popular of the methods because it buys you very little. In this method, the direction of the detail has a good orientation for eye sockets, but not much else. Like with the first example, the mouth will be problematic because the detail will bunch up in the corners of the mouth. The neck will also need to be seamed. Still, a skilled modeler can make a very convincing face using this method.

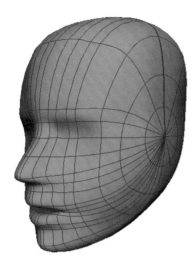

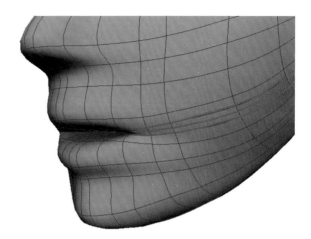

With the poles at the ears, the direction of the detail has a good orientation for the nose and brow,

The extra detail needed to make a mouth cavity causes the splines to bunch up at the corner of the mouth.

Which Topology to Use?

There are many opinions as to which topology is best when constructing a single surface head out of a sphere. The best way to choose is to evaluate your character and its needs.

If your character needs to talk, or move its mouth at all, place the pole at the mouth. This makes the mouth far more controllable, though there is a bit of a trade-off when it comes to attaching the head to the body. This, however, is a much easier problem to deal with than a poorly built mouth.

If your character doesn't talk or move its mouth, other topologies can be used. Having the pole at the top of the head is probably the second choice because it enables a seamless neck, which can make attaching the head to the body less complicated.

Placing the pole at the ears offers the fewest advantages of the three. Not only is the mouth hard to control, but the neck must be seamed as well.

Exercise #1: Modeling a Simple Head

This exercise shows you how to create a basic head out of a sphere. Because we want this character to talk, it is modeled with the pole at the mouth. This gives you a radial mouth that animates quite well.

This particular head was modeled using NURBS patches, but the same techniques could be used to model a polygonal head. The head being modeled is fairly realistic. Don't let this deter your imagination. The same basic structure can be used for a wide variety of heads—both real and stylized.

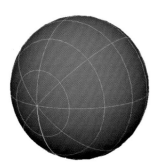

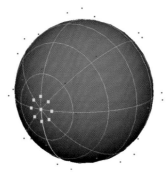

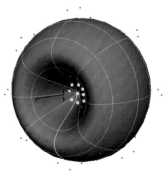

1. Start with a simple sphere with approximately 8 sub-divisions in either direction. Position the pole so that it is facing forward.

2. Select the vertices on the front part of the sphere.

3. Pull these points straight back to create a hollow mouth cavity inside the head.

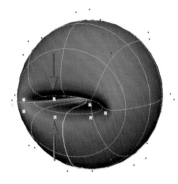

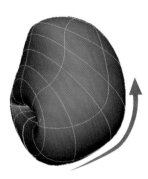

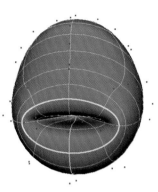

4. Select the vertices around the lips and scale them down vertically. You now have the beginnings of the character's lips.

5. For this particular head, we will sweep the detail up so that there is a pole at the top rear of the head and another at the back of the throat. Select each row of vertices, and then move and rotate them so that the detail sweeps up and back. Reshape the head as needed.

6. After you have a basic shape blocked out, start adding detail. Start by adding a few rows of vertices near the lips.

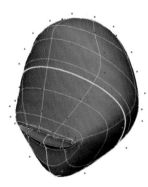

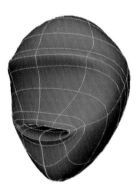

7. Sculpt the added detail to make the lips more realistic. At this point, just try to get the basic edges of the lips defined. More detail will be added later.

8. Add a few rows of vertices near the brow.

9. Again, sculpt out the brow. How prominent you make it will depend on the design of your character, but try to get the basic detail running horizontally.

continues

Exercise: continued

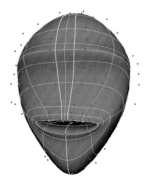 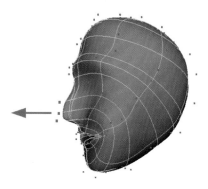 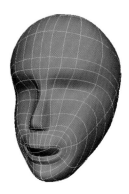

10. Now for the nose. Add columns of vertices on either side of the vertical center.

11. Pull out the vertices residing just above the lips to create the nose. (This new detail can also be used to flesh out the top lip.) The exact shape of the nose will be dictated by your character's design. More complex noses may require that more detail be added.

12. After the nose is blocked out, you're halfway there. The rest of the work is simply tweaking the shape and adding extra detail where necessary. Getting the shape exactly right requires time, patience and a good eye. If you decide to add new detail, do it gradually to keep the surface smooth.

More Complex Heads

Heads made by deforming a sphere are quite flexible, and can be turned into a wide variety of shapes. This type of head, however, always has trade-offs. The detail around the mouth may need to be changed to accommodate the eyes or the neck. This can prove frustrating for more demanding characters.

In this case, a more complex head may need to be built. This can be accomplished in a number of ways. The simplest is to model the head as a polygonal surface and use subdivision to get it smooth.

Another way is to build the surface of the head out of multiple surfaces. The eye sockets, for example, may be built out of a separate surface and blended on a sphere-based head. This can avert some of the topological limitations of the spherical head.

The face may also be built out of multiple patches seamed together. Depending on the software chosen, this technique may be more complex, but the basic topology is similar to that of a polygonal head.

Modeling a Polygonal Head

Polygonal heads may be either simple or complex. The big advantage to a polygonal head is topological freedom. This enables you to arrange the detail so that it works best in each area. Unlike a sphere-based head, a polygonal head does not need to compromise the mouth detail to accommodate the eyes or the neck.

This particular model demonstrates this point, The mouth on this character is radial, much like in the previous exercise. The eyes and brows, however, are not compromised. Like the mouth, each eye has a radial topology. The brow is naturally horizontal, which makes it easier to sculpt and animate.

Exercise #2: Building a Polygonal Head

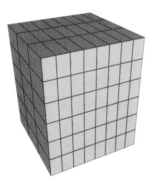 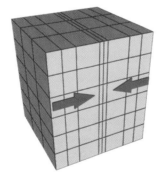 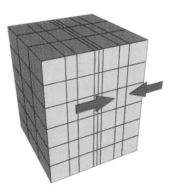

1. Start with a simple cube. This particular cube has 7 rows and 5 columns of vertices, and is 3 rows deep.

2. Start by moving the detail around on the face of the cube. It is easier to manipulate the detail on a flat surface, so the head is kept as a cube while all the detail is added. First, take the two columns of vertices on either side of center and move them together.

3. Move the detail on the left side of the center together. Do the same for the right.

continues

Exercise: continued

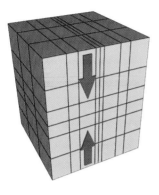

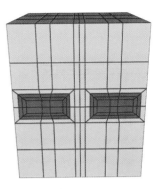

4. Take the two rows on either side of the center and move them closer together.

5. Now make some eye detail. Select the polygons near where the eyes will be and inset them. If you don't have an inset command, you can bevel or extrude the faces and then move the faces back so that they are flat with the rest of the cube.

6. Repeat this operation a few times to get enough detail so that you can sculpt the eyes.

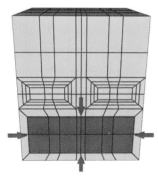

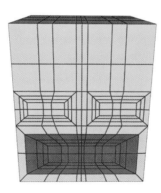

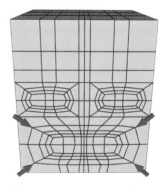

7. Create detail for the mouth. Select the two rows of polygons beneath the eyes and inset them. If your modeler does not have an inset function, extrude or bevel the faces out and then move back the faces so that they are flat with the rest of the cube.

8. Repeat this operation a few more times to get enough detail to sculpt the mouth.

9. Select the corners of the mouth and scale the vertices inward to round off the outline of the mouth. (If you look closely, this detail will look a great deal like the radial mouth created in the previous exercise.) Round off the corners of each eye in the same manner.

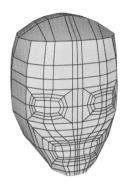

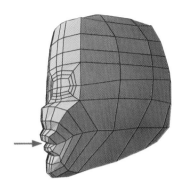

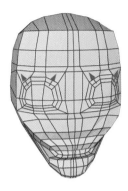

10. Up until now, the head has been a cube, which made it easy to add the required detail. After the detail is in place, sculpt the cube into a more headlike shape. This can be done using a number of tools, such as a lattice or another type of deformer. It can also be done the old-fashioned way, by tugging vertices.

11. Work on the profile of the face. Pull out the cheeks, and sculpt the lips (arrow).

12. Start sculpting the eyes. Push the detail along the top of the eye up to create a brow ridge. Sculpt the brow from this detail. Reshape the eyes to match your character's design.

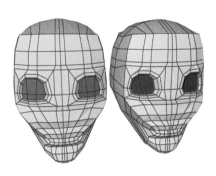

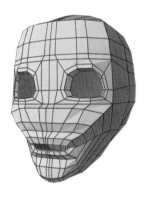

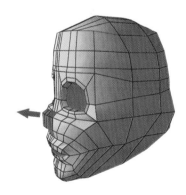

13. Create eye sockets by selecting the polygons inside the eyelids and extruding them inward. You may also choose to delete these polygons (right) to create holes for the eyes.

14. Create the mouth cavity by selecting the polygons along the inside of the lips and extruding them inward.

15. Create the nose by selecting the polygons above the lips and extruding them outward.

continues

Exercise: continued

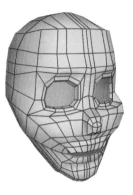 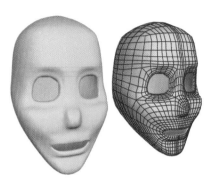

16. Round out the nose to the desired shape. Finish sculpting the rest of the face to match your character's design.

17. When the low-resolution version is complete, it can be subdivided to create the high-resolution version.

Eyes

Eyes are one of the most expressive areas of the face, so it's essential to have eyes that are controllable in every respect. Eyes tend to fall into two broad categories: internal and external.

Internal

Eyes internal to the head give a realistic look when rendered. An eyeball is really just a simple sphere or hemisphere.

Internal eyes are akin to realistic eyes. The eyelids are part of the facial surface, with the eyeball inside the skull. If your character design dictates internal eyes, you plan for this by modeling eye sockets when constructing the head. This was done on the polygonal model that was constructed in this chapter. For a NURBS model, one way to do this is to create a little pouch for the eyeball to sit in. This, however, can add a lot of detail that may get you at animation time. Another way is to trim out the eye socket and then blend a second surface for the eyelids to the original head.

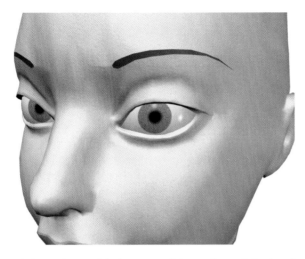
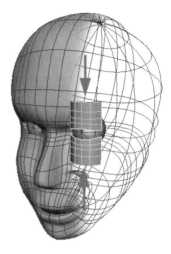

The lids can be modeled as part of the surface of the head.

The lids can also be separate objects, such as a hemisphere or these shutters that show only when the eyes blink.

The eyeball itself can be either a sphere or a hemisphere, because only the front part of the eye will ever show through the skin. The pupil can be made with a simple texture map or a second hemisphere sitting on the first.

The big problem with internal eyes is that you need to keep the eyeballs locked in the socket while the head moves. This is usually accomplished with a hierarchy—the head being the parent of the eyes. Another issue is the movement of the eyelids. They must move along an arc that's the same radius as the eye. This can be done using a multiple-target–morphing utility. It also can be accomplished by animating the lids using clusters or some other form of direct manipulation.

Another way to create lids for internal eyes is to model a separate lid that animates and remains hidden until the eyes close. For fast eye closures, such as blinks, this can be fine, but if the lid is closed too long, the audience may pick up the seam where the separate lid pokes through the skin.

External

External eyes are separate objects made from spheres or cylinders that sit on the surface of the face. They can have a more cartoonlike appearance, and are easier to control than internal eyes. Because they don't have to line up exactly with the eye sockets on the face, you have much greater freedom over how they're placed. They're great for Tex Avery–style eye-popping and afford the animator a variety of stylistic choices.

Eyes external to the head are made of spheres that sit on the surface of the face. They work well for stylized characters.

External eyes can be exaggerated wildly to get a cartoonish look.

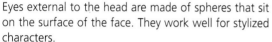

Exercise #3: Modeling Eyes

Eyes are easy to make and can be made from any type of geometry. These can be used as internal or external eyes with the heads you made earlier.

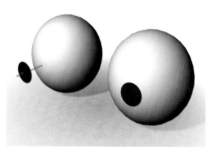

1. Start with a simple sphere. This will be the eyeball.

2. Create the pupil. This can be done by creating a very shallow hemisphere with a slightly larger radius than the eyeball, but which shares the same center. The pupil will glide above the eyeball much like a contact lens.

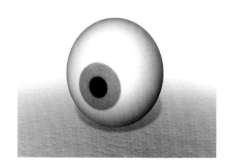

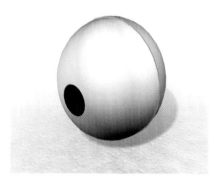

3. Alternatively, the pupil can be created as a texture that is mapped directly to the eyeball. For a complex eye, you can have two maps on two meshes: one for the iris, another with transparent edges for the pupil. The mapping coordinates of the pupil can then be scaled to make it dilate.

4. The lid is created in much the same way as the pupil. It is a half-hemisphere slightly larger than the eyeball.

5. Fit the lid so that it shares the same center as the eyeball. Next, set up the hierarchy so that the eyeball parents the pupil and the lid.

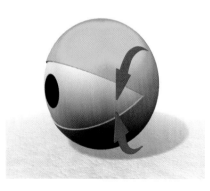

6. A second lid can be created by duplicating the first.

7. The eye can be blinked simply by rotating the lids.

Asymmetrical Eyes

Most realistic characters will have spherical eyes like those created in the previous exercise. A stylized character, however, may need eyes that are oblong or asymmetrical. This can be accomplished in a number of ways. For oblong eyes, you can use a trick that depends on how hierarchies work. If the eyeball parents the lid and pupil, the eyeball can be scaled either vertically or horizontally. Because the lids and the pupil are children of the eyeball, they inherit the scaling, allowing them to move perfectly along the surface, even though the eyeball is nonspherical. The scaling can also be animated to give a squash-and-stretch effect.

You can take this concept one step further with the use of a lattice. Applying the lattice to the entire eyeball hierarchy enables you to distort the shape of the eyes even more. Because the lattice distorts the entire hierarchy, the lids still move along the eyeball's surface. The lattice can also be animated to give a very cartoonish effect.

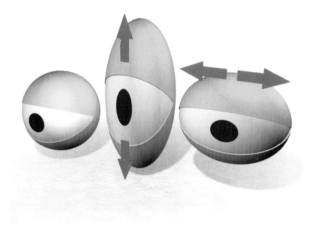

Oblong eyes can be created by scaling the eye vertically or horizontally.

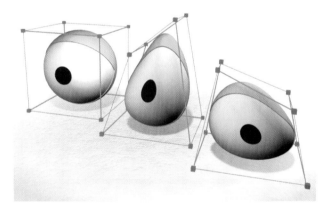

Applying a simple lattice to the eyeball hierarchy enables you to distort the shape of the eyes to get cartoonish shapes, while still allowing the lids to blink.

Eyebrows

Eyebrows go a long way when you are trying to animate emotion, so be sure to plan for them when designing your characters. Depending on the design of your face, the eyebrows can be modeled as part of the surface of the face or as separate objects.

Brows can be modeled by creating a brow ridge that runs across the tops of the eyes and the bridge of the nose.

Eyebrow hair can be painted on as a texture. You can also go further by creating geometry to represent the individual hairs.

This dog's eyebrows are separate objects that float above his head. They are very stylized, but can be moved much more easily.

Eyebrows that are part of the surface of the face can be modeled by creating a brow ridge that runs horizontally across the tops of the eyes and the bridge of the nose. How prominent the ridge becomes depends on a number of factors. A large, lumbering character may have a very heavy brow, for example, but an infant would have a very subtle brow. After the brow is modeled, you can create eyebrow hair along the brow ridge. These can be painted on as a texture. You can also go further by creating geometry to represent the individual hairs.

Eyebrows separate from the face are less realistic, but can take a wider variety of shapes and positions. These can be constructed from a variety of shapes and can float free or ride along the surface of the forehead. You can animate the eyebrows using any number of methods, including shape animation, clusters, lattices, or a skeletal deformation system.

Teeth

Because teeth are rigid objects, they are fairly easy to construct out of polygons, but they certainly can be constructed of patches as well. Basically, teeth are rectangular in shape and slightly rounded at the corners. Teeth can be constructed individually and grouped together in a hierarchy or constructed as one solid object. Teeth are slightly curved and should be modeled to follow the inside of the skull and jaw.

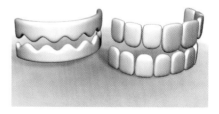

Teeth can be modeled as a solid object or a tooth at a time.

Teeth are not usually modeled as part of the head, but are placed inside the surface of the head behind the lips. Because we usually don't model a skull or a jaw, the teeth are the audience's only clue for this underlying structure. To maintain believability, it's best to move the teeth the same way they're moved in real life.

In real life, top teeth are attached to the skull and do not move in relation to the head as a whole. To get this effect digitally, simply use the head as a parent and don't move the top teeth. Bottom teeth are attached to the jaw and rotate along with it when the mouth opens. One way to assure this is to make the bottom teeth pivot around the same axis that the jaw rotates. This is located slightly in front of and below the ear. That way, the lower teeth can give a good impression of a true jaw.

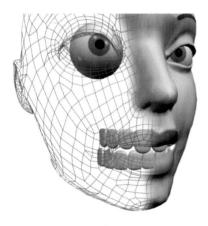

Teeth are not usually modeled as part of the head, but are placed inside the surface of the head behind the lips.

If you want, you can also model gums for your character.

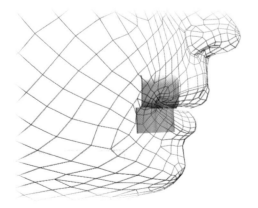
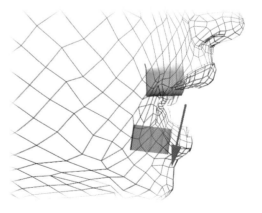

The top teeth are stable to the skull.

The bottom teeth rotate with the jaw.

Tongues

The tongue is important when animating speech, though not as critical as some may think. Most of the characters in *Toy Story,* for example, did not have tongues. Still, it's nice for your character to have a tongue, to add an extra bit of realism.

The tongue is a very flexible object and can be animated with a skeletal deformation system, a lattice, a cluster, or some other form of shape animation. The tongue is typically a separate object that floats inside the mouth cavity. Because we rarely fly our digital camera down our character's throat, the back of the tongue is rarely seen.

The easiest way to build a tongue is by squashing a sphere and putting a dent down its length. Texture and bump maps can also be used to make a more detailed surface. It's a good idea to fade this texture to black at the back of the tongue so that the back of the tongue remains hidden.

A tongue in three easy steps: A sphere is created, then it's squashed, and then a dent is modeled down the middle.

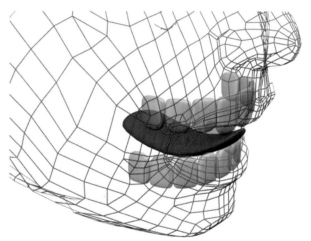

Typically, the tongue is a separate object that floats inside the mouth cavity.

Connecting a Head and a Body

After you've made the head, you create a neck and attach it to the body. There are three basic ways to do this.

Neck on the Body

You can model a neck as a small protuberance from the body and simply place the head over it. This gives you a bit of a seam where the head connects. For those who model with NURBS, a blend can be used to help hide the seam where the head hits the neck.

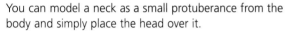

You can model a neck as a small protuberance from the body and simply place the head over it.

A NURBS blend can also be used to help hide the seam where the head hits the neck.

Neck on the Head

You can also extrude a neck from the head and attach it to the body at the shoulders. This is good, because it leaves no seam on the open skin of the head and neck. The seam of the neck and body can be better hidden on the shoulders or underneath a piece of clothing. For a patch-based surface, the surface of the neck can also be attached to the body, using tools that keep the surfaces locked together.

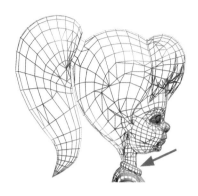

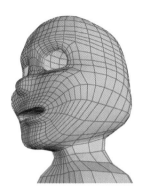

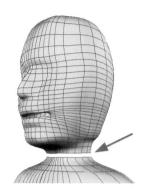

Keeping the neck as part of the head enables you to hide the seam on the shoulder or beneath a collar or other bit of clothing.

For polygonal models, connecting the head to the body is relatively simple.

A seamless connection for a NURBS-based character requires that the detail of the head and neck line up.

Head, Neck, and Body as One Object

For a completely seamless connection, the head can be modeled as a part of the torso. For polygonal models, this is relatively easy. Many times, the head is built from polygons extruded from the body. Conversely, the body can be constructed by extruding polygons from the lower part of a head. The vertices of the body can also be attached by welding vertices together and building faces that span the two objects. A number of packages have automated tools to help with this task.

For NURBS-based characters, a seamless connection means planning the topology of both the head and torso so that they are open at the neck. Additionally, the detail lines of both need to line up exactly. A head with the pole at the top of the head is a good candidate for this type of connection. A head with a radial mouth can also be used, but only if the detail is swept down to leave an open neck.

Conclusion

With the character's head firmly attached to the body, you should have constructed at least one complete character. When you've finished your character's head and attached it to the body, you should be ready to begin animation. The next few chapters discuss setup and animation of the body, with the final chapter on facial animation.

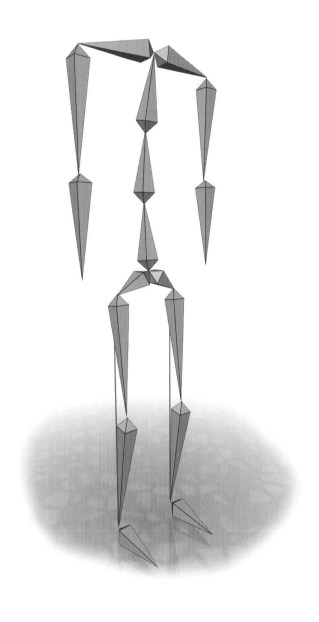

CHAPTER 6

Skeletons and Mesh Deformation

After your character is modeled, you get it ready for animation. If your character is fully segmented, this may mean joining the segments into one hierarchy. If your character is partially segmented, or if it's a single-skinned character, you deform the skin. Typically, this is done using a skeletal deformation system.

In a skeletal deformation system, the skeleton is what is actually animated. This makes setting up the skeleton a critical phase in the character-building process. A properly built skeleton can be quickly and easily manipulated to attain any pose. In this chapter, we concern ourselves with basic setups. After the skeleton is built, it will, in turn, deform the character. When rendered, the character will hopefully look alive to the audience.

Hierarchies and Character Animation

Depending on how you designed your character, you have either a collection of segments or a single skin to be deformed by a skeletal deformation system. Either way, you need to find a way to connect the segments and/or skeleton into a cohesive character. You want the hand to move with the arm and the legs to move with the hips. You can glue your character together in this manner using a hierarchy.

A hierarchy is simply a way to tell the computer how the parts of your character are linked. Taken literally, the hierarchy tells the computer the foot bone is connected to the shin bone, the shin bone connected to the thigh bone, and so on. Technically, the hierarchy looks a bit like a tree, with each connection forming a branch. It can also be thought of as similar to the nested directories and folders found on your computer. The foot is a subfolder of the shin, the shin a subfolder of the thigh, and so on.

Manipulating Hierarchies

When manipulating a hierarchy, moving the parents moves the children. This is also known as forward kinematics. In an inverse kinematics environment, the opposite happens—the children drive the parents. This is discussed a little bit later.

In a forward kinematics environment, if you move a child object—a twig, for example—you won't move the parent—a branch or the trunk. But, if you move the trunk, everything else, including branches and twigs, follow along. Just like a tree, a hierarchy must have a trunk, a single parent that controls all the other branches. The same follows for a character's body. In a human skeleton, the trunk is almost always the hips or pelvis. The pelvis is close to the center of gravity of the human body, which makes it a good candidate for a parent. More importantly, it is the center weight distribution for the entire body.

The hips support the spine and the entire upper body, passing this weight down to the legs. This makes the spine and legs children of the hips. In turn, the spine parents the shoulders, which have the arms as their children, and the legs parent the feet. Having the trunk, or the root of the hierarchy, at the hip area helps you create motion such as a back flip, for example, because that rotation is dependent upon the rotation of the hips.

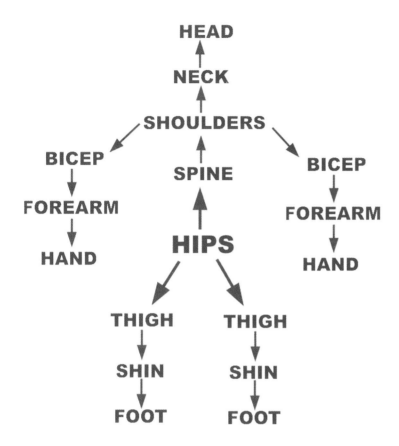

The basic hierarchy of a human body. The hips are the parent of all joints. If you move the hips, the rest of the body follows.

Not all setups have everything linked in one single hierarchy. There are times when you need to create a broken hierarchy. This actually keeps some of the joints separate to aid in animation. A character in a dress, for example, might have the legs as separate objects, which could exist in a separate hierarchy. Another example might be an extremely simple character, such as a flour sack, where the leg skeleton is only one joint. In this case, it might be easier to keep the legs outside the hierarchy.

Pivots and Joint Rotation

When assembling a skeleton or segmented character, you need to tell your software how the joints of your character's body rotate. The shin, for example, rotates about the knee. When you create an object, such as a model of a shin, the computer has no way of knowing it's supposed to be a shin, and no way of knowing that it rotates about the knee. It simply assigns the pivot to an arbitrary point—typically, the physical center of the object.

The forearm is rotating around its default pivot point—the center of the object. Real forearms rotate.

To make the forearm rotate properly, you need to manually reassign the pivot so the forearm rotates at the elbow.

Unfortunately, in character animation, arbitrary points are not acceptable. As you assemble your character, you may also need to move the pivots on your joints so that everything moves properly. The forearm rotates around the elbow, the thigh rotates at the hip, the head pivots at the neck, and so on.

Exercise #1: Building a Simple Segmented Character

This exercise builds a segmented character out of spheres and cylinders. It can be constructed in almost any package. The character is simple, but it is designed to show how a basic hierarchy is put together.

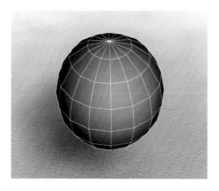

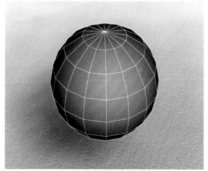

1. Start with a sphere.

2. Select the polygons on the top of the sphere.

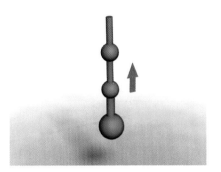

3. Extrude these faces upward. This will create a simple ball-and-stick shape that will be used for the joints of the character.

4. Adjust the pivot of this segment so that it matches the center of the sphere.

5. Copy the first joint twice. Place the copies end-to-end, as shown, to create a basic spine. Make the base of the spine the parent of the middle segment, the middle segment the parent of the top.

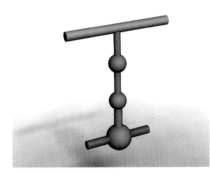

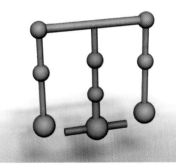

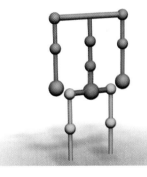

6. Create two cylinders. One represents the hips and is placed at the base of the spine. Make this segment the parent of the spine base. The top cylinder represents the shoulders, and is the child of the top of the spine.

7. Hang two more ball-and-stick joints off each side of the shoulders to make arms. The shoulders parent the biceps, which in turn parent the forearms. Simple spheres at the end of the forearms can act as very simple hands.

8. Copy the arm segments and translate them down to the hips. Make the hips parents of the thighs, and each thigh the parent of its corresponding shin.

continues

Exercise #1: continued

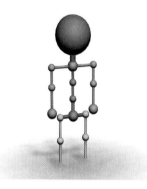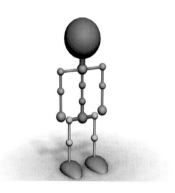

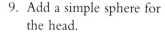

9. Add a simple sphere for the head.

10. Add two flattened spheres for the feet.

If the hierarchy is constructed properly, moving the hips should move the rest of the body. Rotating the thigh should move the shin and foot. If the pivots are in the right place, all the joints should rotate around the sphere at the base. Move your character around the screen and test the rotations on all the joints. Put this character aside for later exercises.

Skeletons and Hierarchies

Single-skin characters do not have segments, so their meshes must be deformed. In this situation, the skeleton is most often used as the deformer. The skeleton is built from bones and joints, objects that are usually tetrahedral in shape and do not render. They fit inside a single-skin character much like real bones, and then the skeleton is connected in a hierarchy much as in the previous exercise. Bones typically don't render, which is fine because they are really only helper objects. They simply act as a guide for the mesh deformation utility, telling the utility where to move the mesh. This is discussed a bit later.

Many software packages also enable skeletons to be made of regular objects. These objects can be any type of geometry, but most people simply use boxes because they are easy to model. As with bones, the boxes act as guides for the mesh deformation plug-in. Because regular objects are visible to the renderer, these objects must either be hidden or have their rendering attributes switched off before the character is rendered.

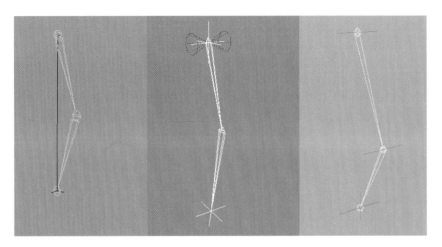

Bones are created in several different software packages. Even though the bones look slightly different, the packages all work pretty much the same.

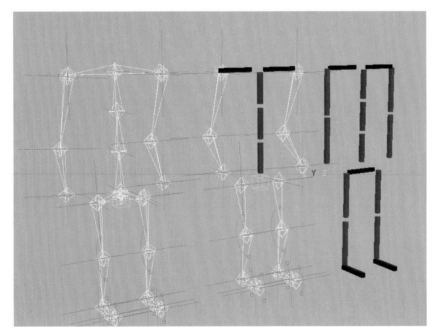

In addition to bones, many packages enable other types of geometry to be used in a skeleton. Here, we have a skeleton made of bones, one made of bones and boxes, and one made of just boxes. All can be used to deform a mesh.

Manipulating Hierarchies

When a character or skeleton is connected using a hierarchy, the joints can be manipulated. There are two strategies for doing this: forward kinematics and inverse kinematics. As you will see, each has its own disadvantages and advantages. Many characters are built so that some parts are manipulated using forward kinematics and other parts using inverse kinematics.

Forward Kinematics

Forward kinematics (FK) manipulates the character from the top of the hierarchy down. This is what you did to test the character in the previous exercise. If you move the pelvis, the whole body moves; if you rotate the elbow, only the hand moves. When you use forward kinematics, you soon realize that, with the exception of the pelvis, rotating your character's joints is the only way to move the body parts around.

If you want to place a character's hand on a coffee cup, for example, you first rotate the shoulder, then the elbow, then the wrist and fingers, working your way from the top of the hierarchy down. Each rotation brings the hand closer to the cup. You can't simply pick up the hand and place it on the cup, because the arm will not follow.

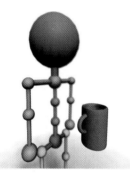

1. Placing this character's hand on the cup using forward kinematics is an exercise in rotations.

2. First, rotate the arm at the shoulder.

3. Next, rotate the arm at the elbow to meet the cup. When working with a character using forward kinematics, you work from the top of the hierarchy down.

Inverse Kinematics

Inverse kinematics (IK) is simply another way of manipulating a character. If set up correctly, it can be an animator's dream. It is the exact opposite of forward kinematics, because moving the children rotates the parents. Inverse kinematics is simple to use: You place the character's hand on the coffee cup, and the rest of the arm automatically follows the cup when you move it. This simple action is more complex that you think, however, because the software must solve the rotations for all the joints so that everything looks natural. Luckily, most advanced software has features to assist IK, such as a damping function that softens the motion as the joint approaches its limit.

One disadvantage of IK is that you get only one key for the whole hierarchy, because each joint's motion is being driven by an end effector. For two jointed limbs, such as human arms and legs, this may not be a problem, but in a many-jointed limb, such as a tail, you lose control over the limb's shape. In this case, FK may be the best bet.

When positioning the hand with inverse kinematics, the hand is simply pulled to the coffee cup and the rest of the arm follows.

The computer doesn't know how the joints of the body are supposed to move. If it's just as easy to bend the elbow backward or sideways to solve the problem, that's fine with the computer. Unfortunately for the animator, backward-bending elbows are neither a natural nor accepted solution. Elbows are a hinged joint that can bend only forward. Without this information, the computer can't position the joints properly

Here are three different ways to rotate the joints so that the hand rests on the cup. Only the first of these solutions is correct, but the computer doesn't know that. You need to tell the computer exactly how you want your joints to behave.

Creating IK Chains

In order for the computer to position the joints properly, it needs to know a bit of information. First, it needs to know how many bones, or joints, are in the chain, as well as their respective lengths. This is typically done when creating the joints on the computer. As the joints are drawn, a hierarchy is created automatically within the software.

The first joint in the chain is known as the *root*. It's also the root of the hierarchy. It may also contain data helpful for the positioning of the chain, depending on the software. Moving the root moves the entire chain. When drawing a chain, always start with the uppermost joint in the hierarchy. If you are drawing a leg, for example, start with the hip and work down to the ankle and foot.

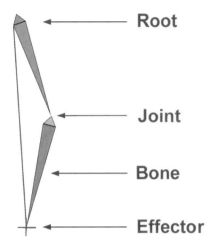

Root

Joint

Bone

Effector

The parts of an IK chain.

The tip of the last joint of the chain is known as the *effector*. The effector controls the position of the end of the IK chain. The software always tries to position the chain so that it runs between the root and the effector.

Between the root and the effector are bones connected by joints. These are simply articulated points in the chain. An arm has one joint—the elbow—and a spine may have many joints.

Manipulating a Chain

The chain is manipulated through the use of the effector. As the effector is moved, the joints of the chain rotate to meet the effector. This makes posing and animating a character easy, because you need to consider only the position of one effector rather than the rotation of many joints. You give up some of the control you had with FK, but, in return, you can animate with ease, much like working with a puppet. In fact, some studios call the low-res version of the skeleton "the puppet."

What happens when you pull the effector beyond the limits of the joints? Most software keeps the joints at a fixed length, so the fully extended chain aims itself at the effector. Some software, however, can enable the joints to stretch, expanding their length of the entire chain to meet the effector. This sort of effect can be good for squash-and-stretch. Squash-and-stretch on bones enables a large foot to pass under a short body by stretching the leg as the foot passes, for example.

At the other end of the chain, translating the root typically moves the entire chain, including the effector. This is because, hierarchically, the effector is a child of the root. This means that when the root moves, the effector moves. Here's an example: If your IK chain is a character's

Translating the effector bends the IK chain.

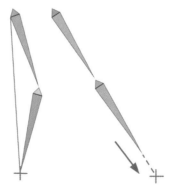

When the effector is moved beyond the limits of the chain, the chain simply aims itself at the effector.

If the root is moved, however, the entire chain, including the effector, also moves.

leg, the root is the hip and the effector is the foot. If you move the top of the leg, the foot moves as well. This is not the way to set up a skeleton if you want the feet to remain fixed to the floor.

Constraints

To get around this problem, many packages use a device called a *constraint*. A constraint tells one object to stick to another object. If you constrained a ball to a box, moving the box also moves the ball. On the surface, a constraint seems to work the same as a hierarchical link. You could just as easily parent the box to the ball to get the same result—moving the parent (the box) would move the child (the ball). The difference is that a constraint operates outside any hierarchy.

Many skeletons constrain the effector to an object outside the leg hierarchy. Because this outside object does not move with the root, it remains fixed in space. The effector, in turn, remains fixed to the outside object. This enables the root of the chain and the effector to be moved independently, which makes posing the character much easier.

A constraint is used to stick the effector to the box. Because the box is outside the hierarchy, the effector remains in the same place, even when the root is moved.

Joint Limits

To prevent elbows (and knees) from bending backward, you need to inform the software exactly what the limits are for any given joint. Most packages enable this to be configured on a joint-by-joint basis. Some packages have different types of joints—you can specify a joint as either hinged (two-dimensional) or ball-and-socket (three-dimensional).

Rest Positions and Goals

Many packages now have incorporated the idea of a default position, also known as a rest position or a goal, for a series of skeleton joints. This forces the chain to return to the default shape when the effector is moved to its default position. Typically, this is the position that the joints were first created, but some packages enable this position to be redefined at any time.

This feature helps considerably because it makes the behavior of the skeleton quite predictable. It is also exceptionally good for chains with many joints, such as an animal's tail.

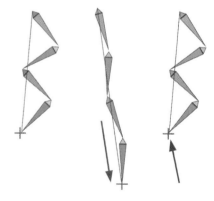

A rest position always returns the chain to the same shape when the effector is in the same place.

Real Time and Calculated IK

In the past, most machines simply weren't fast enough to solve IK equations in real-time. This meant that the equations had to be solved in a separate pass, which "baked" the joint rotations into the joints. Most desktop machines today are fast enough so this is no longer a limitation.

As such, most 3D packages offer real-time IK, which simply means that the equations are solved in real-time. This greatly enhances interactivity and posing of the character.

There are times, however, when you may still need to calculate the IK solutions and bake in the joint rotations. Most of these situations involve transporting the animation to other places. One good example is in video gaming. Most game engines accept only rotational data, forcing you to bake in the IK solutions. Those using a third-party renderer may also need to solve IK in order for the animation to be properly managed.

Which Kinematics to Use?

As you can see, inverse kinematics systems have a few more options, which make them a bit more complex to set up. After they're set up, however, animation is much faster. Forward kinematics, on the other hand, is very straightforward. The question of which technique to use depends on each individual part of the skeleton.

Forward kinematics is most commonly used in the upper body. The spine, shoulders, and arms can be animated using forward kinematics. If a character is standing and gesturing with his hands, this works just fine. If he takes his hat off and throws it, touches another character on the shoulder, holds hands with another character, or basically interacts with anything else, IK may be required. The spine and hands are usually animated with FK, though IK can be used.

One place where IK is almost always used is the legs and feet. IK is ideal for keeping a character's feet locked to the ground. If the character is swimming, however, FK may need to be used on the legs and feet, as well as the arms. As you can see, many times the choice of one type of kinematics over the other depends on the specific demands of the shot. To get around this, many productions have more than one setup for a character. Which particular setup gets used depends on the task at hand.

Building Skeletons

Building a skeleton is similar to putting together a segmented character. The big difference is in the use of IK chains, as well as constraints. The next two exercises build a skeleton for a body and for a hand.

Building a Body Skeleton

The skeleton for a body should be built with your mesh as a reference. It is often a good idea to place the bones inside the mesh as you build the skeleton to ensure a perfect fit. Some people have been known to build generic skeletons and fit them to mesh after it's built. This technique, however, can cause a problem when scaling the bones to fit the mesh.

Exercise #2: Creating a Skeleton with Your Mesh

1. Build your skeleton inside your character's mesh, using the mesh as a reference.

2. Start with the legs. Draw a simple IK chain with two joints. The mesh has been removed here, but make sure the knee of the chain aligns with the knee of the mesh.

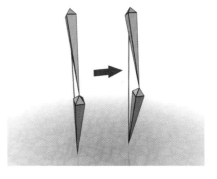

3. Copy the first leg to make a second. Align the second to the mesh.

4. Draw two bones to create a pelvis. Make the pelvis the parents of the legs.

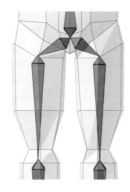

5. When viewed with the mesh, the pelvis and legs should look something like this.

6. Draw three bones to create a spine. The pelvis should be the parent of the lowest vertebrae.

continues

Exercise: continued

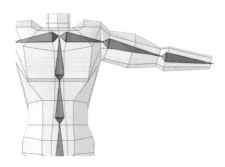

7. At the top of the spine, cre-ate two bones for the shoul-ders. Make the top of the spine the parent of the shoulders.

8. Draw an arm and link it to the shoulder. Copy this to make the other arm.

9. When viewed inside the mesh, the upper body should look something like this. Make sure the shoulders attach to the arms above the armpit, not inside the torso.

10. Add feet to the body. These can be single joints or, to better articulate the foot, two joints per foot.

11. If you are using IK, set up the constraints. Create a null or dummy object near the right foot. You can also use other objects if you desire, such as text or a nonrender-ing box. Constrain the ankle to the object (arrow).

12. When the constraint is acti-vated, the leg should snap to the object. Moving the object will now manipulate the leg. Move the leg back to a neutral position. Repeat the procedure for the other leg. If you want to use IK on the arms, repeat the proce-dure for the arms as well.

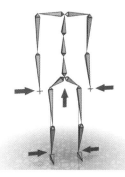 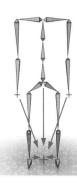

13. When all the constraints are in place, manipulating the body is accomplished by moving five objects: the hips, the leg constraints, and the arm constraints. One problem with this setup is that, to move the entire body within the scene, you need to move all five objects.

14. This can be overcome by adding one more null or dummy object and making it the parent of the hips, leg constraints, and arm constraints. This keeps the legs, arms, and hips at the same level, while keeping all the character's parts within a single hierarchy.

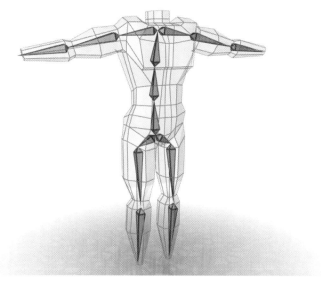

15. The final skeleton should fit nicely within the body.

Hand Skeleton

Skeletons for hands are reasonably straightforward. It is simply a matter of creating one bone per finger bone, plus an extra set of bones for the palm. As with a skeleton for the body, it's always best to build the hand skeleton inside the hand mesh.

Exercise #3: Building Hands

1. Start with a bone stretching from the base of the palm to the middle of the first knuckle.

2. Create three bones for the first finger. Align the bones so they run through the center of the finger and the joints line up with finger joints.

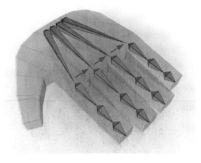

3. Repeat the procedure for the rest of the fingers.

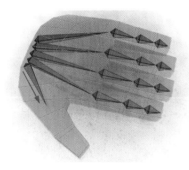

4. Now make the thumb. Draw a bone that stretches from the base of the palm to the middle of the thumb's knuckle.

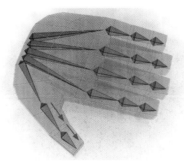

5. Then draw the two joints for the thumb itself. The skeleton is now done. The hand skeleton is attached to the wrist simply though a hierarchical link.

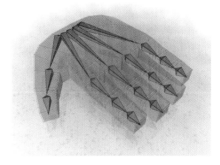

6. The final skeleton can be attached to the arm of your character through a simple hierarchical link.

Mesh Deformation

After a skeleton is built, it can be used to deform the skin of your character. This is done through a mesh deformation utility, which uses the position of the bones to determine the shape of the mesh. As the bones of the skeleton are animated, the skin of the character also animates. How this is done depends on your software and its capabilities. Most packages use a combination of methods, but they fall into the general categories of direct assignment and envelopes.

Direct Assignment

Direct assignment is the simplest method of deforming a character. In this method, each vertex in the model is assigned to its corresponding bone or joint. The vertices in the thigh are assigned to the thigh bone, those in the shin assigned to the shin bone, and so forth. For simple models with few vertices, this method is quite easy and predictable. Because the calculations are easy, deformation is usually reasonably fast, making the character easy to manipulate in near–real-time. Most software does this automatically, assigning each vertex to its closest joint, though some packages may force you to do the assignment manually. If the software assigns the vertices automatically, there is usually some manual cleanup anyway to manage vertices assigned to the wrong joint.

Another way to accomplish this task is to create clusters for each part of the body (that is, a cluster for the left thigh, another for the right thigh, and so forth) and assign each cluster to a joint. This is done either through a simple hierarchical link or via a constraint or expression. Make sure if you do this that all the joints and/or bones are named accordingly, because the clusters will be named that way too, and it will be confusing if you do not name them right in the first place.

The one problem with direct assignment is that it will not produce truly organic results. This is because most parts of the body are affected by more than one joint. For example, the knee is affected by both the shin and the thigh. Directly assigning those joints may cause tears or creases if they are moved to extremes. Still, for basic characters, direct assignment is simple and works quite well.

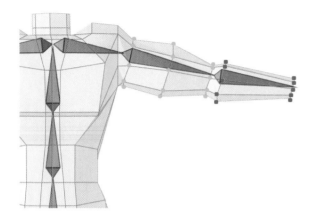

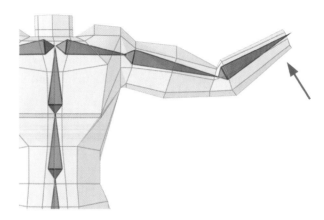

Direct assignment links the vertices in the mesh directly to the skeleton. In this example, the vertices in the forearm (red) are assigned to the forearm bone. The vertices in the upper arm (green) are assigned to the upper arm bone.

When the forearm moves, the mesh deforms to match its motion.

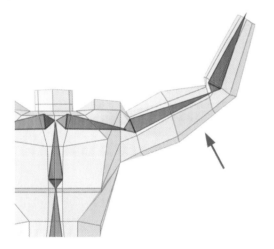

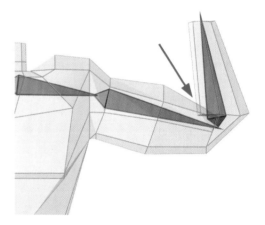

When the upper arm moves, it moves its vertices. Because the forearm is a child of the upper arm, it moves too, as do its vertices.

The big problem with direct assignment occurs when the joints move to their extremes. In this case, the motion of the forearm causes the vertices surrounding the elbow to severely crease.

Weighted Assignment/Envelopes

For a more organic deformation, you may need a vertex to be affected by more than one joint. The vertices around the elbow, for example, can be affected by both the upper and lower arm. This brings in the concept of a weighted deformation.

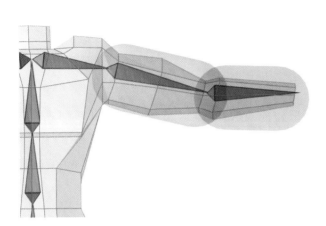

An envelope is basically a range of influence. Where the envelopes overlap, the vertices are affected accordingly.

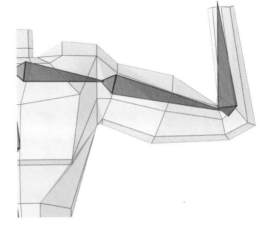

When the arm bends, the vertices around the elbow are weighted according to their envelopes, which eliminates the crease.

A weighted deformation enables more than one joint to affect a given vertex. How this is done also may vary, depending on the software. Many packages have a visual reference, typically known as an *envelope*. An envelope is basically a range of influence. Where the envelopes overlap, the vertices are affected accordingly.

Some software also enables numeric weighting of clusters. A given cluster, for example, can be affected 70% by joint A and 30% by joint B. In practice, this is similar to envelopes, but can be more flexible, because the vertex assignments are not constricted to a specific area. You could theoretically assign any vertex to any bone with any weight. Of course, without the visual reference, it is certainly a bit more difficult to set up.

The cluster method is much less visual than envelopes, which are displayed by bubblelike icons that can show what is being included in the deformation. Many packages overcome this by coloring the vertices according to their weight. This can act as a visual reference, easing setup.

More advanced envelope systems enable you to move the control points of the envelope's bubble to include or exclude the stray vertices. The one problem that might crop up with simpler implementations of an envelope-based system is that you may not have the capability to reshape the envelope. This gives you no way to deal with stray vertices. A good example might be the fingers in a hand—the envelopes for one finger might overlap and affect the vertices in another. If your software doesn't allow you to customize envelopes, you can avoid these sorts of problems with clever modeling. You might model the fingers farther apart than in the normal relaxed hand to keep the envelopes from overlapping, and then move the bones back into a relaxed position after the deformation is applied.

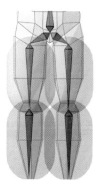

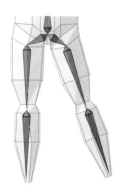

The envelopes in these legs overlap slightly at the knees, which is good, but this also causes the right leg's envelopes to overlap the left's.

When the thigh rotates out, the vertices from one leg are still affected by the other.

To fix this, either the envelopes need to be reshaped, or vertices on one leg need to be excluded from the other.

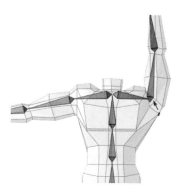

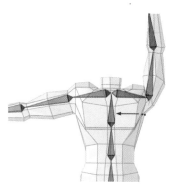

Another common problem is the area underneath the arms. Typically, vertices in this region get assigned to the closest joint, in this case, the upper arm. This causes a telltale bulge as the arm is raised above the head, because these vertices rotate out from the body with the arm.

The vertices under the arm are part of the torso and are affected more by the spine than by the arm. Reassigning these vertices to the spine helps avert the problem and eliminates the bulge.

Advanced Deformation Tools

One step beyond weighted envelopes are tools that enable you to control the shape of the envelope, based upon the position and angle of the joint. These tools are aimed at simulating advanced effects, such as bulging muscles and stretching skin. These tools are great for gaining an extra edge when it comes to realism, and can also be used for other types of effects. They are not, however, absolutely essential when it comes to learning the art of animation.

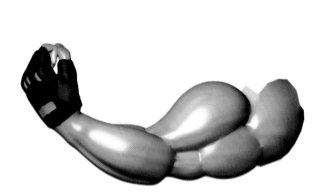

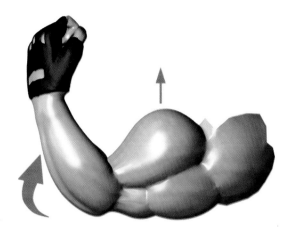

Advanced deformation systems enable you to define how the shape changes as the angle of the joint changes. Here, we have an arm with lots of muscles.

As the skeleton bends the arm, the biceps bulge like real muscles.

Deformation and Surface Type

Typically, most mesh deformation tools work the same regardless of the geometry type. The tool simply takes control of the vertices on the model, moving them along with the joint to deform the character. Whether those vertices belong to a polygonal, patch, or other type of surface really doesn't matter much to the software. Polygonal and patch models, however, do have a few unique issues that need to be addressed.

Deforming Polygons

Low-resolution polygonal surfaces deform quite easily, but do not look good when rendered. Conversely, a high-resolution polygonal surface renders well, but can be a real pain to deform. As pointed out in Chapter 2, "Modeling Basics," the solution is to deform a low-resolution version of your character, and then subdivide the surface after it has been deformed, rendering the high-resolution model. If your software supports this type of functionality, it is simply a matter of dialing up the resolution before the animation is rendered.

If your software does not support subdivision after deformation, the solution will be different. In this case, the animator will manipulate and animate a low-resolution stand-in model. When the shot is complete, the high-resolution model is swapped in, the animation from the low-res character applied, and the shot rendered.

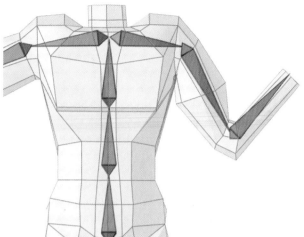

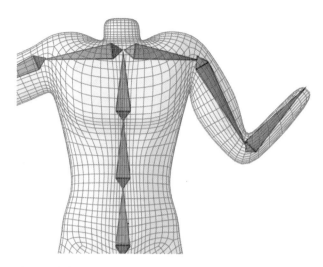

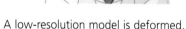
A low-resolution model is deformed.

The model is then subdivided after the deformation. This keeps the model easy to animate, and it makes it smooth when rendered.

This is where enveloping comes in quite handy. If the high-resolution model is simply a smoothed version of the low-resolution model, the envelopes applied to the low-res model should affect the high-res model pretty much the same. This enables you to use the same skeleton and envelopes on both models. When render-time comes around, you simply hide the low-res model and unhide the high-res model.

Of course, theory and real life never quite match up, so you will certainly have many headaches when using this method. Most often, the high-res model will not deform exactly like the low-res model, causing problems. If the hands don't deform exactly the same, it may mean the difference between holding a drink and having the fingers pass through the walls of the glass.

The only way around these problems is to thoroughly test the setup before it goes into production. This is absolutely the most important part of your success. Test the character against a skeleton animated through a wide range of motions. This way, any problems will show up and be able to be managed before animation begins. If the low-res model is as close to the high-res in deformation as you can possibly get it, you will spend less time working on damage control. Some high-end productions have been known to have animators move vertices on a frame-by-frame basis to clean up these sorts of mishaps. This is not, by any means, a pleasant way to spend a week's worth of work.

Deforming Patches

Because patches define surfaces of variable resolution, you do not need to subdivide their surfaces. This means that a patch surface can be rendered directly without fear of jaggies or artifacts. Most patch surfaces are also fairly light, so deformation is usually reasonably fast.

If a character has a lot of detail modeled into its surface, however, a patch-based character can get as complex as a polygonal surface. In this case, you again may need to have two different models: a low-res one for animation and a high-res one for rendering. If you must do this, the issues involved are exactly the same as a polygonal model, so refer to the previous section.

For a NURBS-based patch surface, you will find that the most problems are with the blends. Blends are a calculated surface that automatically changes shape to fill in the gap between two other surfaces. If these two other surfaces exhibit a great deal of motion, the blend may break up or cause kinks. It's always best to keep the blend outside the principal range of motion for a joint. As mentioned in Chapter 3, "Modeling Basics for Animation," don't put the blend right on the shoulder. Instead, place it on the torso to lessen the strain on the blend.

Another thing that must be mentioned is that blends take quite a bit of computing power to calculate. It is always a good idea to hide your blend surfaces while animating. It will eliminate these costly calculations and speed up your interaction with your character.

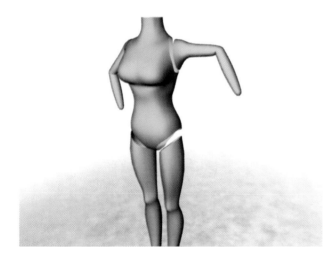

When animating a character with NURBS blends, hide the blends for increased speed.

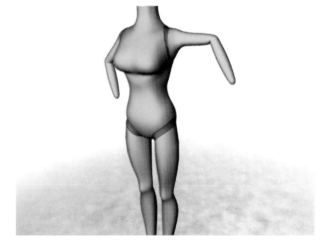

When the animation is finished, unhide the blends.

Skeletons and Segmented Characters

If your character is made of segments, or partially segmented, you still can use a skeleton to manipulate it. The individual segments can be hierarchically linked to the corresponding joint in the skeleton. Manipulating the skeleton will then move the joints.

This technique is redundant for joints manipulated using forward kinematics, because they can just as easily be manipulated directly. For those joints that need inverse kinematics, however, this technique can work quite well.

Other Deformation Methods

Skeletons are not the only way to deform a character. There are plenty of other options available to the animator. Most of these methods are used to deform parts of a character, but they can also be used for entire characters, if necessary.

Lattices

One of the more popular tools is the lattice. A lattice is simply an array of points, usually box-shaped, that surround a character or a part of a character. Moving the points on the lattice will, in turn, move the region of the character surrounded by the lattice.

Lattices have many uses. As you saw in Chapter 5, "Modeling Heads for Animation," lattices can be used as an aid to facial animation, particularly for cartoon eyes. They also can be used for things like muscle bulging. For simple characters, such as a flour sack, the lattice may be all you need to deform a character.

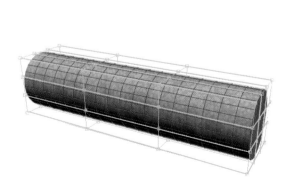

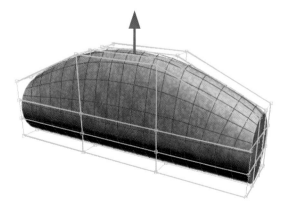

A lattice is placed around this cylinder.   When the lattice is moved, the vertices on the cylinder follow.

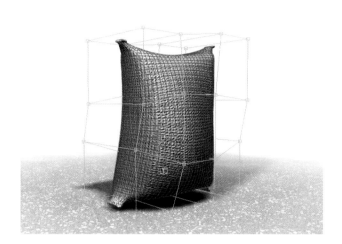

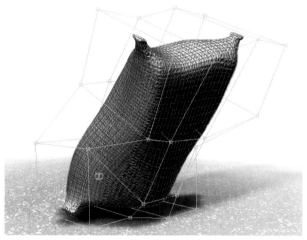

Lattices can also be used for animation. This flour sack is deformed using a simple lattice.

Animating the shape of the lattice animates the shape of the flour sack.

Clusters

Clusters are another way to animate the shape of your character. In its simplest sense, a cluster is a collection of vertices. This enables you to control many vertices with just one cluster. More complex systems enable you to weight vertices between several clusters, which can give you a very sophisticated deformation system.

Clusters are used in a number of places. A cluster linked to a skeleton can be used as a skeletal deformation system. Clusters can be used to simulate effects such as muscle bulging. Some people use clusters to control parts of the face—for example, the eyebrows or the tongue—in facial animation.

Spline Deformation

Spline deformation enables a simple spline to control the shape of an object. Animating the vertices of the controlling spline can animate the object. One good example where this technique might be used is in an animal's tail. Another place it might be used is in a character who has a ponytail.

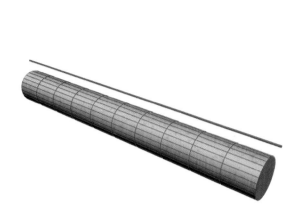

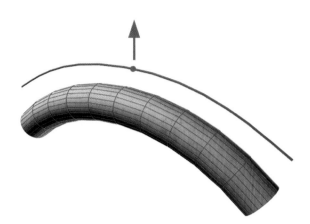

The spline just above this cylinder is used to control its shape.

Move one vertex of the spline, and the cylider changes shape to match.

Morphing

Morphing enables one object to assume the shape of another. Morphing is most commonly used in the area of facial animation. Because the face is such a complex shape, it is best to sculpt the many individual poses a character's face may take. This enables precise control of the specific shapes. A morphing utility enables you to smoothly animate between these shapes.

Multiple target morphing enables multiple shapes to be mixed and blended to create new shapes. For facial animation, this enables even more control over the shape of the face, because the extremes can be mixed and blended in any ratio or combination. Facial setup and animation is covered in depth later in the book.

Conclusion

As you can see, skeletons and mesh deformation can help you bring a solid mesh character to life. Although many packages have tools that are similar in the way they work, there are many package-specific differences that you need to consider when deforming your own character. This means cracking open the manual for the little tricks that are unique to your chosen software.

For those just learning animation, these tools can get very complex, so try not to get too bogged down in the fine-tuning of your character's deformations. If your character is overly complex, you can spend more time setting up a character than you do animating it. It is better for the beginner to create a simple character that deforms easily rather than a complex character that is difficult to control.

Always remember that the goal of a good setup is to make the character easy to animate. If your character is hard to animate, you will take much longer to learn the craft. The best idea is to invest the time needed for the setup to make your job easier when you animate. You don't want to be "duct-taping" your animation together because it wasn't set up right in the first place.

CHAPTER 7

Posing Characters

Now that you've built a few characters, you can start on the fundamentals of animation. Before you actually move your characters, however, you need to understand where and how they will be moving. Specifically, you need to understand how your characters are going to be posed—exactly how they will stand, sit, or walk in relation to the camera. A pose is a fundamental building block of animation, and many animators block out a character's major poses while animating.

Posing determines, to a great extent, how your audiences perceive the characters and their emotions.

Intimately involved with posing is the concept of staging. This determines where your characters are in relation to the camera, their environment, and each other. Again, these relationships determine exactly how your animation plays to the audience. Until you understand how to place your characters properly in front of the camera, it makes no sense to move them. So, let's look at the basics of posing.

Posing

A pose is simply the way a character presents itself to the camera. If the character is sad, happy, frightened or brave, you should be able to read that emotion in its pose—the way the character stands, where its hands are placed, the position of its head. Every part of the body has a role in creating the pose. Theater, dance, mime, and countless other performing arts involve posing to a great extent. Similarly, animation is another art form that relies heavily on clear poses and silhouettes to convey a message.

When animated, your characters need to show emotion. Even the simplest shots require a character to hit a strong pose. Whether the character is sad, happy, proud, or surprised, the emotion shows in the body and the pose.

A simple character can show a great deal of emotion simply through the pose of the body.

Animating with Poses

In the golden age of animation, animators discovered there are two basic methods for animating a scene: straight-ahead and pose-to-pose. Each method uses posing differently and has its own place and its own advantages.

Pose-to-Pose Animation

Pose-to-pose animation is the more controlled of the two. In this method, you plan your shot and get the main poses of the character within the shot blocked out. If your character is standing up from a chair, for example, the poses may be leaning back, grabbing the armrest for support, leaning forward, and, finally, standing up. A character winning the lottery may read the lottery ticket and then show disbelief, shock, and joy. The theory is that every action can be broken down into a series of distinct poses. From there, it's a matter of creating in-betweens or letting the computer in-between the poses for you —and, of course, tweaking these as necessary. It is a good way to animate difficult and tightly choreographed shots, as well as slower subtle pantomime moves, because those do not have many surprises or quick motions to them. Pose-to-pose animation is also good for dialogue, because each pose can be fit to the major points in the dialogue track. The downfall of the method is that it may lack spontaneity.

Straight-Ahead Animation

Straight-ahead animation is pretty much what the name implies. In this method, you start on frame one and animate "straight ahead" from there. This method is more improvisational in nature and can sometimes lead to very spontaneous and complex motion. It's also a great method for quicker action motions because of the spontaneity. Straight-ahead is the method closest to "acting" a frame at a time, and it is very similar to the techniques used in stop-motion animation. If you are trying to achieve a stop-motion look and feel to your animation, this is certainly the way to go. Still, this method can make it hard to achieve well-defined and solid poses, sometimes making animation that is hard to "read." It also makes animating complex shots difficult.

Combining the Two Methods

You can, however, combine the two methods and get the best of both. Computer animation gives you the bonus of being able to do this rather easily. Most fast machines can play back an animation test almost instantly. This makes it easy for the animator to block out a series of poses rather quickly, almost in a straight-ahead fashion, or animate a frame at a time in those sections that might need more spontaneity.

The question that still remains, however, is one of thought process. How do you approach animating your scene? Do you plan your shot carefully (pose-to-pose) or do you improvise (straight-ahead)? This is not an easy question to answer, and the best advice is to use your intuition and experience. Overplanning a shot may very well sap the life out of it. Being more improvisational can add unexpected touches and details you would have never dreamed of. On the other hand, complex shots need to be planned very carefully or all the elements simply won't sync up.

When you combine the two methods, you plan the extreme poses and then tighten that up with straight-ahead interpretation between those poses. The first part lays the groundwork, and the second part spices it up and gives it life, leaving behind all the computer interpolation that makes an animation look mechanical. With a computer, you can easily use both. I highly recommend you use both techniques to get a good animation; if you rely on just one or the other, you easily see where their weaknesses are.

Posing a Flour Sack

One easy character to use to begin studying posing is a simple flour sack. This little character has become a classic tool for the study of animation. The flour sack is simple to construct, but it has volume and weight and can be easily posed.

How a flour sack relates to a human body may be a bit confusing to the newcomer. The easiest way to conceptualize this connection is that each corner of the sack represents the arms and legs of the character. Of course, these are very stubby arms and legs. Another way to think of the character is that the corners of the sack are the hips and shoulders of the character. This is a bit more accurate and leads you to a better understanding of how the body works. Almost all motion in the body starts at the hips and then translates to the limbs. This is also how you should pose characters—from the center of the body outward.

If you pose the hips, spine, and shoulders properly, the arms and legs will be much easier to position naturally. This is because almost all motion begins at the hips and continues down the tree of your skeleton. The only time this changes is when a character is reacting from being hit or pulled with or by something. When the character is interacting with something else, this rule changes to lead with whatever part of the body is being hit or pulled.

A simple flour sack is a good character to pose.

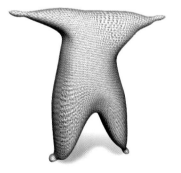

If the corners of the sack are stretched, you can see how they can be thought of as arms and legs.

If separate arms and legs are added, you can see how the corners of the sack can also be thought of as hips and shoulders.

Setting Up a Flour Sack

The flour sack can be deformed using any number of methods. Some people use a simple method, such as a rectangular lattice. The points of the lattice are deformed, which reshapes the sack into the desired pose. A simple skeleton, without arms and legs, can also be used. A skeleton is good, particularly for learning, because it lends itself to an understanding of the underlying anatomy.

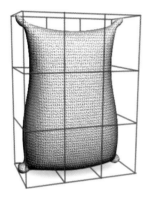 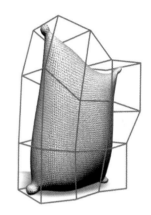

A flour sack can be deformed using a simple lattice.

It can also be deformed using a simple skeleton and a mesh deformation tool.

Posing the Sack

After the sack is modeled and deformed, the task of posing the sack is simply a matter of manipulating the skeleton, lattice, or other type of deformer to get the pose you want. When posing the sack, try to make the poses convey emotion and meaning.

Exercise #1: Posing the Flour Sack

On the CD is a flour sack model ready to be deformed. Set it up in your favorite package and use it to create a dozen or so interesting poses.

As inspiration, here's a few to get you started:

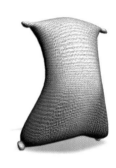

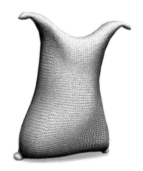

Posing Characters

Now that you've had a bit of practice posing a simple character, you can move to a more complex character, such as a human body. When posing a human body, you need to understand anatomy, the skeleton, and how they all tie together. (Much of this was covered in Chapter 3, "Modeling Bodies for Animation.") This knowledge will help you create strong poses. Strong poses are one of the fundamental building blocks of animation. They're read well the instant they're viewed. If your poses are strong, the audience knows exactly what's happening and will under-stand your character's actions better. Also, a good pose is almost always balanced, giving your digital characters the distinct feeling of weight and life.

Balance

Keeping a pose balanced is very important. The body is simply a system of joints that is trying to stay in balance. Each bone acts as a tiny lever, distributing the weight of the body through the spine to the hips, and then down through the legs to the ground. If a pose is out of balance, the character will appear as if it's about to tip over. If the body is slightly out of balance, the eye will still pick it up and see the pose as wrong without an apparent reason.

This is an unnatural pose. Rarely does the body rest equally on both feet.

Placing the weight on one leg, however, forces the hips to lean. This puts the body out of balance, making it look like it's about to tip over.

Twisting the spine so the shoulders are turned opposite to the hips places the body in balance.

In the human body, all balance starts with the hips. The spine and the upper body rest on the hips, and the hips rest on the legs. Any forces generated by the legs reach the upper body through the hips. The hips are also close to the center of gravity of the body and thus are close to the center of most motions.

Because everything stems from the hips, they're the best places to start when posing a character. In a relaxed stance, the body usually rests on one leg, not both. If you've ever watched people waiting in a long line, you'll know what I mean. People constantly shift their weight from one foot to another as they wait. Rarely do they place their weight equally on both feet, except when standing at attention. As the poses get more complex, you need to pay attention to balance very closely. If a character picks up an object, for example, the object's weight should be balanced by the rest of the body. When a person rests on one leg, it throws the whole system off center. When the weight is on one leg, the free leg pulls the hip down and out of balance. This, in turn, curves the spine and forces the shoulders in the opposite direction to maintain balance. If the body is about to move forward, the shoulder may drop on the same side as the hip. Either way, the body's natural state of balance is asymmetrical.

Symmetry

Because the body is so symmetrical, it is very tempting to place it into symmetrical poses. Not only is this dull and boring, it is very unnatural. To keep your characters looking natural, you need to keep them asymmetrical in almost every way—from the positions of the eyes, hands, and feet to the motions and actions that they do. Symmetry has this odd habit of creeping in at the worst times.

Avoiding symmetry means avoiding what animators call twins. A *twin* is simply a part of the body that mirrors another. Even minor details in a pose—such as both feet pointing in the same direction—can make a character look strange.

This pose is symmetrical in almost every respect. It is also boring in almost every respect.

This pose breaks symmetry in a number of places.

And so does this one. Both of them are more interesting and look more natural.

This character is locked in a very symmetrical pose. This is full of twins, such as the legs and arms, and it is not very interesting.

Rotating the hips forces the spine to twist to maintain balance and makes the pose asymmetrical. This makes the character look more natural.

Weight

Another point to consider is the weight of the character as well as the weight of everything else in the scene. Consider a character standing on the edge of a diving board. A heavy character will bend the diving board considerably, and a tiny character will hardly bend the board at all. A character lifting a heavy suitcase will need to lean its body away from the suitcase to get it off the ground.

How heavy is the bag? Until the character lifts it, we do not know.

This bag is very light. You can tell this by the pose.

This bag is very heavy. Again, the pose gives us the information.

Another important point to consider is the weight of the character itself. Skinny characters have no problem supporting their own weight. In a hurricane, however, they may tend to blow away. Heavier characters, on the other hand, will be more stable in hurricanes, but may have problems supporting their own weight when they are simply standing. This can cause the knees of a heavy character to bend outward to support the extra weight. Be sure to take these factors into consideration when posing your characters.

When animated, a heavy character moves much slower than a light character and needs a lot of force to begin moving. Think of a dinosaur —it needs momentum to get moving. But a mosquito is quick and light and needs barely any momentum to get moving.

Staging

When a character is posed, the pose must still be presented to the audience. You must always remember that your 3D animated creation is almost always going to be shown on a 2D screen. The screen is your stage, with the audience viewing everything through the camera. As such, your characters must present their actions clearly to the camera so that the audience can read and understand them well.

Probably the best way to pose characters for the camera is by studying methods pioneered by magicians, mimes, and stage actors over the centuries. Good silhouettes and a strong line of action help present your characters to the camera properly.

Creating Strong Silhouettes

One of the most important fundamentals is presenting a strong silhouette to the audience—or, in our case, the camera. The human eye first picks out the silhouette of an object and then fills in the rest of the detail. If the action is presented so that its outline is clear, the action will be much clearer as well.

Think of a magician pulling a rabbit out of a hat. He always pulls the rabbit out to his right or his left. This way, even the person in the back row can understand what's going on. If the magician wants to hide something, he'll usually do it when his hands are passing in front of his body. The body, along with the motions, serves to conceal the action. The same principles apply to animation. Animators usually don't have to worry about performing sleight of hand, but they're very concerned about making actions read. The silhouette is the key.

A good silhouette will tell you what this character is doing...   ...he's about to pull something from his hat. If the silhouette reads, so does the pose.

To check out your character's silhouette, simply pose your character in the computer. Next, apply a matte black texture to the character. Render the pose. You'll have nothing but the silhouette. Another way to go about it is to simply look at the alpha channel matte used to composite the character into the shot—it's always the silhouette.

When you have this image, ask yourself, "What is this character doing?" If your silhouette is clear, the action and the pose will read.

A good example of silhouetting is this kick. The image reads well both as an image and in silhouette.

Turn the camera 90 degrees, however, and nothing reads. The angle from which you view your character is as important as the pose itself.

Line of Action

In addition to a strong silhouette, a good pose should also have a definite line of action. This is a strong line that you can follow from your character's feet to the tip of its fingers. This not only makes your pose more effective, it also adds beauty to the pose. The human eye is naturally drawn to a good line.

For example, if your character is throwing a ball, arch the back and make the arm follow along the same arc. This gives a much more pleasing line than if the arm just moves back. If you put the whole body into the throw, it looks more convincing.

This pose is weak because it has a weak line of action.

Getting the character's whole body into the action creates a stronger line of action, as well as a stronger pose.

If a character is in a tug-of-war, he digs his heels into the ground and arches his back, putting every muscle he can into the effort. Even simple actions should follow a definite line. If a character is proud, he arches his back and throws out his chest. If he's tired, he slumps over and has a completely different arc.

This tug-of-war pose shows a great line of action.

If a character is tired, he slumps over in a different line of action.

Staging Multiple Characters

Not only does the animator need to know where to place the characters in relation to the camera, but also where to place the characters in relation to one another. How do you make them interact and read?

The solution depends on a study of acting and interpersonal relationships. Characters who are friendly can be staged closer than characters who are enemies. Every situation has its own demands. For example, a marine drill sergeant intimidates a recruit by yelling at him a few slim inches from his face. Lovers who are angry at each other turn away and stand practically back to back.

How you place the characters depends on the dramatic requirements of the scene as well. If you want to highlight a character's facial expression, place that character so the camera is closer to his face. Similarly, if you want to make a character seem distant and alone, place him off in the distance. Placing characters at different distances from the camera also gives your shot more depth and makes your film more dynamic.

These stagings might work for a simple conversation.

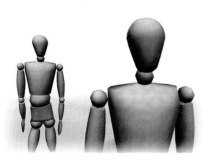
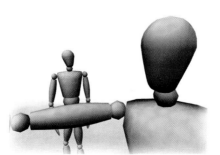

To get more depth or to highlight one character over the other, different stagings may be required.

When you have more than two characters in a scene, use the composition to direct the eye to what's important. Think of the characters as weights. If you put one character off to the side of the screen, you may need several toward the center of the shot to keep it balanced. If you have too many characters on one side of the screen, the shot will lose its balance and look odd. If the shot requires the characters to be toward one side of the screen, other items, such as furniture or foliage, can be used to help balance the composition.

Characters, particularly crowds, can also be used as a way to frame what's important in the shot. Remember that the composition affects how the audience interprets the scene. For example, think of those times where a crowd parts to reveal the hero, or those shots where a gang of people surrounds the villain. A crowd is a shape that can be animated in its own right. Use this tool in your compositions as well.

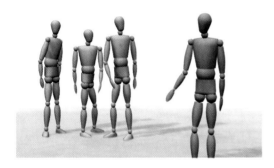

Think of your characters as weights. In this poorly staged shot, the three characters on the left tilt the weight of the composition to the left.

To balance things out, bring the isolated character closer to the camera to make him bigger and give him more weight. This makes the shot more pleasing.

Characters can also be used to frame the action. Here, the characters in the crowd are used to frame the character in the distance.

Looking a bit deeper, notice how the heads of the characters form a "V" shape, which leads the eye directly to the central character. The shape of the crowd is a handy composition tool.

Staging and Camera Placement

Proper camera placement is important for anyone involved in film. Knowing where to place the characters in relation to other characters, the camera, and the environment is essential to achieve the maximum dramatic effect. Placing the character in just the right place at the right time is an art that every director needs to master. A good example of proper camera placement is a simple example. What if you have a character dangling from a rope over a deep crevasse?

If you aim the camera from the side, the audience will not know that the character is in danger.

Pointing the camera down into the pit reveals the danger.

Another important factor in staging is how the camera position affects the perception of the shot. When the camera is placed low and is shooting up at a character, it makes him seem more menacing. Think of any 1950's sci-fi movie where the giant insect is menacing a major metropolis, and you'll get the idea. Conversely, keeping the camera high makes characters seem helpless and insignificant, much like ants when viewed from above.

Moving the Camera

Computer animation makes it extremely easy to move the camera. Computer animators probably move their cameras far more often than necessary. For spaceship flybys and architectural walk-throughs, this may be great; but for character animators, this can spell instant disaster—especially when you are trying to present an action, feeling, or emotion to the camera. When the camera moves, the motion draws attention away from the actors and toward the camera. Because moving the camera effectively changes the pose, it also forces you to rethink your poses every time the camera moves.

Still, moving the camera can be very effective when it's done at the right time and for the right reasons. Panning with a running character gives the feeling of motion. A rack focus blurs the background or foreground, giving strong emphasis to another part of the scene. You may want to move in the camera quickly in a moment of fear. These all are simple tricks that live-action directors have used for decades. Remember the most important thing: As with motion blur, you should never notice it. The camera should embellish the scene, but never move so much that it becomes a character in itself.

In a digital environment, you can easily place several cameras in a scene to get the equivalent of the live-action, three-camera shoot. Use one lens for the establishing shot, one for the action, and one for the close-up. Even in 3D, lenses tend to have different effects. Many live-action directors shoot close-ups with a longer lens, because it flattens the perspective and focuses attention on the actor. On a panoramic shot, the director may use a shorter, wide-angle lens to get as much of the landscape as possible into the shot.

The same goes for 3D. Instead of just using one lens and moving the camera, change the field of view to get different effects. As with live action, try to keep the lens the same for the duration of a shot, and change lenses only after a cut. Changing the field of view within a shot is typically not done in live action, and it is not a good idea for most character animation, either. Again, do not draw attention to the camera.

For those whose 3D shots are composited with live action, knowledge of the lenses used in the live-action shoot is critical. For animators who use software without stock lenses, the lens length is equivalent to the angle of the camera's field of view (FOV). The wider the FOV, the shorter the lens. These values are shown in Table 7.1.

Table 7.1 Conversion between the Lens Length and the Camera Field of View

Lens	Field of view	Type of lens
15 mm	115.0 degrees	Ultra Wide Angle
20 mm	94.286 degrees	Very Wide Angle
28 mm	76.364 degrees	Wide Angle
35 mm	63.0 degrees	Medium Wide Angle
50 mm	46.0 degrees	Normal/Standard
85 mm	28.0 degrees	Medium Long

Lens	Field of view	Type of lens
135 mm	18.0 degrees	Long/Telephoto
200 mm	12.0 degrees	Extra Long/Super

Here's an example of how lens choice affects the composition of a shot:

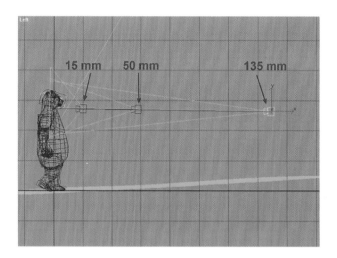

The same pose rendered through three lenses: 15mm, 50mm, and 135mm. The longer the lens, the tighter the angle and the further back the camera needs to be to frame the shot.

Through a 15mm lens, the bear is distorted for a fish-eye effect. Also notice how the landscape is included in the shot. A lens this short might not be so good for close-ups, but it's great for panoramic shots.

A 50mm lens eliminates the fish-eye effect and causes the landscape to recede a bit. The 50mm lens is a good all-around lens.

A 135mm lens flattens the character even more, practically eliminating the background. The 135mm lens is great for close-ups.

Conclusion

This chapter focused on the importance of posing and staging your characters. Remember to keep your poses natural and balanced. Avoid symmetry in your poses and also be sure to keep a strong line of action and silhouette. You must always keep in mind that your audience sees your animation only through the camera, so be sure that you place the camera properly and use the right lenses. As we get into animating your characters in the next chapter, keep these concepts firmly in mind. The best animation will never come across if the camera doesn't see it properly.

CHAPTER 8

The Basics of Character Animation

Y ou are now finally ready to begin animation. As you have seen, animation is more than just moving things around. It involves proper construction of your characters, as well as proper staging and the ability to pose your characters naturally. Now it's time to delve into the nitty-gritty of motion and timing, the heart of animation.

Understanding Newton's laws of motion is certainly one component of the equation. Watching and observing the way people and animals move is another. Watching references—nature films, silent comedies, or classic cartoons—is yet another way to understand motion. It's also important to familiarize yourself with basic animation concepts, such as squash-and-stretch, anticipation, overshoot, follow-through, and many others.

In addition to this, time is a precious quantity that must be used wisely. Timing is a raw material that actors, comedians, and musicians use constantly. A comedian with good comic timing knows exactly when to spring the punch line. An animator who has good timing knows exactly when a character should react, blink, or pull that huge mallet out from behind its back. Timing is the only thing that separates animation from illustration. With proper timing, your characters will appear to live. Without it, they'll look like nothing more than inanimate puppets.

The Importance of Timing

Timing affects every aspect of a film, and on many levels. First, the film is a specific length—from a 30-second commercial to a 2-hour feature. Second, the cutting of the scenes within this time constraint affects the mood and pace of the film. Third, the acting and timing of the character's actions affect how each individual scene plays.

Think of your film as music. Both mediums rely intimately on time. The film is your entire work, much like the song or symphony is a composer's entire work. Your film's scenes can be seen as verses, choruses, or movements. The individual notes of the instruments are the same as the individual actions of your characters. Each action, as in each musical note, must be in the right place at the right time. As in music, bad timing in animation sticks out like a sore thumb.

The Process of Timing

Timing a film starts at the length of the film itself. A commercial may be only 30 seconds, but a feature will be over an hour in length. When this length is known, a storyboard and a script are prepared. The dialogue is then recorded. Dialogue is a big factor in determining how long an animation will take, so use it frugally. Long stretches of dialogue can eat up time very quickly. A slow-talking character can also waste vast amounts of time.

In any event, after the dialogue is recorded, an animatic or leica reel is created to rough out the timing of the whole film. This is accomplished by scanning the storyboard panels into the computer and timing them to the dialogue tracks, using a video editing program such as Adobe Premiere. The goal is to make the film the desired length and to block out the timing for the individual scenes.

After the timing of the shots is blocked out, each shot can then be broken down into the specific actions a character will perform. How this is done depends on the production. Most of the larger, traditional productions use exposure sheets (also known as X-Sheets); most of the newer all-CG shops leave the timing to the animator.

Frames-per-Second and Timing

When you are breaking down a shot for animation, the first issue is the time base, or frames per second, that the production will use. For the first half-century of animation, this issue was simple. All animation was shot to film, and all film ran at 24 frames-per-second.

The proliferation of video, CD-ROM, and other media has clouded this issue. In the U.S., video runs at 30fps; in Europe, it runs at 25fps, and many video games are animated at only 15fps.

With so many time bases being thrown at the animator, it can be difficult to learn how many frames a certain action will take. It used to be that an experienced film animator could tell that a particular action would take a specific number of frames at 24fps. To transfer this knowledge to video, for example, the film animator multiplied this time by 1.2 to get a correct time (24fps × 1.2 = 30fps). Doing this sort of math in your head can be awkward, at best.

With this in mind, what time base do you use for learning your timing skills?

The best advice is to simply learn to time at both 24fps and 30fps, and then you can switch-hit as the project demands. Most high-end productions are still film-based, so this skill will serve you well in this context. Although many animators may work in video or game time bases, 30fps is the proper choice. A good animator's stopwatch might also be a good tool to own, because it can convert to both 24 and 30fps.

Timing Using Exposure Sheets

An *exposure sheet* is simply a sheet of paper with an array of rows and columns. Each horizontal row represents a single frame of animation. Vertical rows contain information, such as the contents of the dialogue track (explained in Chapter 10, "Facial Animation and Dialogue"), camera instructions, and a margin for the director to plan the timing of the shot. This can be done via sketches to explain a character's poses, as well as lines to indicate when the actions start and stop.

An exposure sheet can be used to time animation. Each horizontal row represents one frame of animation.

ACTION	DIALOG	EXP	6	5	4	3	2	1		CAMERA NOTES
		1							1	
		2							2	
		3							3	
		4							4	
		5							5	
		6							6	
		7							7	
		8							8	
		9							9	
		10							10	
		11							11	
		12							12	
		13							13	
		14							14	
		15							15	
		0							16	
		1							17	
		2							18	
		3							19	
		4							20	
		5							21	
		6							22	
		7							23	
		8							24	

Timing on the Computer

Some productions do not use exposure sheets. If this is the case, timing is done directly on the computer by the animator (with the director giving feedback). Most high-end 3D packages allow the dialogue track to be loaded in with the scene data. On a fast machine, this gives the animator the ability to scrub the dialogue in real time, reducing the need for the track to be read manually on an exposure sheet.

Some productions do what is called an animatic, where blocks are placed in the scene and moved about to get a basic idea of how the scene will play. The director then approves the animatic, and the animator uses the animatic as a template to set up the scene and gather the basic timing. It is fairly easy to accomplish, and when played against dialogue, it serves the purpose of the exposure sheet quite well.

How Much Time?

This is the number-one question on every animator's mind: How much time? Time is a very tricky substance. Too much time makes your film slow and boring. Too little time makes your film fast and unclear. As you develop your skills, experience will hone your sense of timing. Trial and error is also a good tool. If you're not sure how long a particular action will take, guess. You can always add frames if the motion is too fast or subtract frames if it's too slow. Computers afford the animator the ability to change timings very quickly.

One Thing at a Time

"One thing at a time" is an important rule in timing for animation. The audience perceives things best sequentially, so you should present your main actions that way—one at a time within a smooth sequence of motions. A character stubs his toe, recoils, and then reacts. If the reaction is too quick, the audience won't have time to read it, so the recoil acts as a bridge between the two main actions.

You must remember that the audience is usually seeing your film for the first time. As the animator, you need to guide the audience and tell your viewers exactly where to look at each point in the film. Think of a *Roadrunner* cartoon. When Wile E. Coyote steps out over the gorge, he takes a while to notice he's suspended in mid-air. He typically reacts and then looks directly at the camera with a pitiful expression. This one drawing can be held for almost a second. He may blink or his whiskers may twitch, but it is essentially a still pose. He then zips off the screen in a few frames. This is a great example, because in the span of time that the pose is held, the audience comes to the same realization as the coyote—he's doomed. It also draws the audience's full attention to the coyote, so when he does fall off screen, they see that clearly as well.

One of the most important lessons you can learn about timing is to draw attention to what is about to move before it moves. An action reads only when the audience is fully focused on it. As the animator, you must guide the audience's eyes only through the character's actions.

Developing Good Timing

A good sense of timing is something that animators develop through years of practice. Observing the world around you is the first step in this process. Breaking down these observations into their exact timing is the next. Many animators dissect classic animated and live-action films frame by frame just to understand the timing. A VCR with a good freeze-frame capability is an excellent investment for an animator to make.

You should dissect live action as much as cartoons, because all motion is based on live action. This is very important to understanding timing. Cartoonish action is an exaggeration of live action. It's sort of like studying life drawing first so you understand the human figure; then, and only then, should you go on to drawing cartoon stuff, or you would never represent the figure correctly with so few lines. This applies to motion, too; if you understand how the body moves in real life, you can sprinkle a little exaggeration onto that to get a cartoonish motion.

Another essential tool is a stopwatch. Whenever you need to time a shot, the first thing you should do is reach for your stopwatch and act out the scene, timing the approximate length of each action. Plug in these amounts as your rough-pose timing and then tweak it in your 3D program. The stopwatch is one of the most important tools an animator can own. It enables you to physically act out your scene and get a fairly good idea of the timing. If you're shy, close the door and draw the blinds, but act out your shots, regardless.

Timing and Software

There are a number of ways to view and manipulate time within a 3D program. These include curves, dope sheets, and paths. Each method has its own strengths and weaknesses, and which tool you use depends on the needs of your shot. Some animators gravitate toward one set of tools over another and have heated debates with other animators over which tool is best. Of course, the choice is personal, so let's go over the main tools that most 3D programs offer.

Curves

Most good animation software presents you with a graphical representation of how your objects are moving. Curves are an invaluable tool for the animator in diagnosing and fixing animation problems. Knowing how to read and manipulate animation curves is an essential skill. Every software package is different, but most curves work in similar ways. Typically, the horizontal axis of the graph represents time, and the vertical axis represents the parameter being changed—position, rotation, scaling, and so on. These parameters are plotted graphically to tell you exactly how an object moves.

Take, for example, a character walking down the street. This motion can be represented as a graph. First, the character may be walking along the sidewalk at a steady rate. The character may slow to a stop at an intersection. When the intersection clears, the character accelerates again to a steady rate of speed.

The motion graph would look something like the figure on the next page.

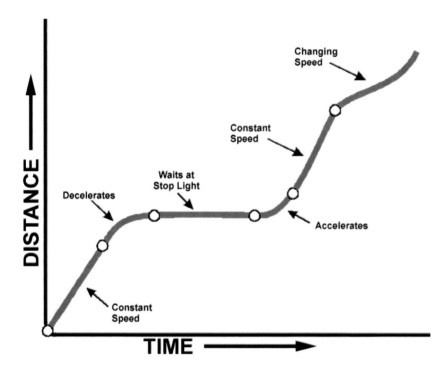

An animation curve of a car in traffic.

When the character is walking at a steady rate of speed, the graph is linear—a straight, diagonal line. When the character is stopped, the change is zero, so the graph is flat. When the character is accelerating, decelerating, or changing its velocity in any way, the result is a curve. A curve that slopes toward vertical represents acceleration, and a curve that slopes toward horizontal represents deceleration.

In most software packages, you have three motion graphs for the object: one apiece for the x, y, and z axes. This way, you can move an object linearly along one axis while giving it variable motion along another.

In this software, red represents the x axis, green represents the y axis, and blue is the z axis. Notice that the blue line is flat, indicating there is no motion along the z axis.

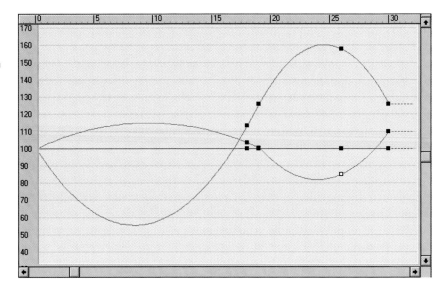

Motion graphs are also good for finding and fixing annoying glitches in your animation. Generally, animation problems show up as distinct spikes in a motion graph. These may be places where a key has been altered, or is in the wrong position. Another use is determining whether something is moving. If you want your character's feet to remain fixed to the floor, the foot's motion graph will also remain flat at the level of the floor.

Here is an animation curve for this character's foot. When the curve is at zero, the foot is flat on the floor.

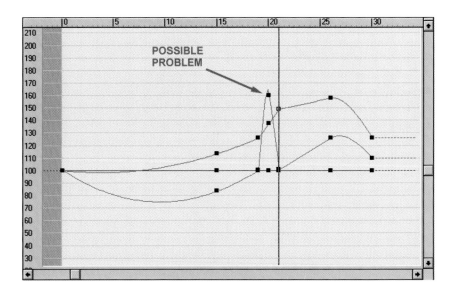

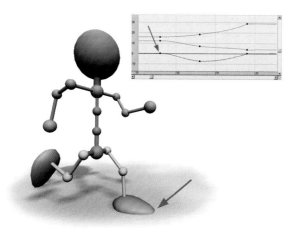

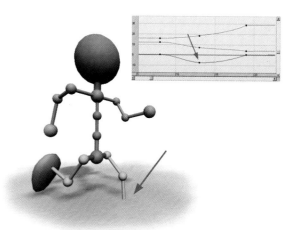

This spike in the curve indicates a sudden change that may cause problems in the final animation.

When the curve dips below zero, so does the foot.

Editing Curves

Editing animation curves is very similar to editing curves used for modeling. Each curve has a control point where each keyframe is placed. Most software will add Bézier-style control handles on the curve to enable you to change the curve's slope. You can also move the control points themselves to change the timing or the value of any particular event.

In addition to Bézier-style handles, many packages also give you other types of default interpolations. A *linear curve* does not do any sort of slow-in or slow-out. A *step curve* looks like a square wave and jumps from one value to the next. Most of these types of interpolations can be derived using the Bézier handles as well.

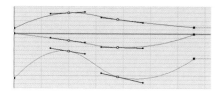

Most curves are manipulated via Bézier handles.

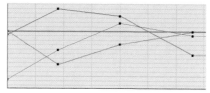

A linear curve has no slow in or out, and thus appears as a series of straight lines.

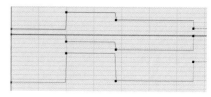

A step curve simply pops from one value to the next, much like a square wave.

Using Curves for Pose-to-Pose Animation

If you decide to animate a shot pose-to-pose, a good knowledge of curves can help you with the process. In cel animation, the poses are drawn first, and then these drawings are timed to get what is called a *pose test*. It is much easier to get the timing of the major poses down before drawing the in-betweens. It also helps the animator focus on the global timing issues without distraction.

The same paradigm can be used for computer animation. In this case, you block out your major poses on the time line using a step curve. This makes your character appear to "pop" from one pose to the next. If a linear or Bézier curve is used, the animation appears "floaty," and the timing is hard to read. Of course, with a character popping from one pose to the next, the animation won't be realistic, but the idea is to concentrate on just the poses and the timing of the poses.

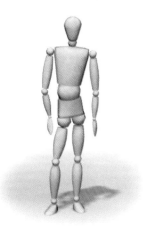

In this simple pose-to-pose animation, the character is standing, leans over to look at the ground, and stands up again.

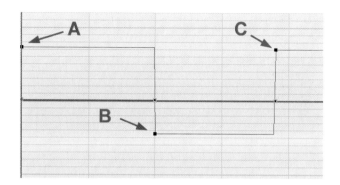

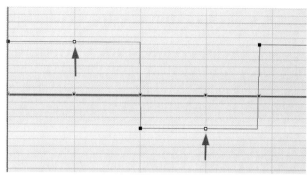

Animating with a step curve makes the character pop between the three poses. This is not realistic, but it is helpful in blocking out the pose timing.

After the timing is set, simply copy the pose keys to a few frames later in the time line.

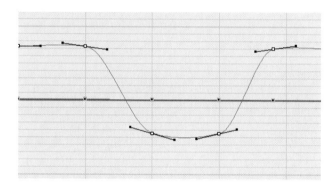

Then change all the curves to Bézier. You now have the character hold a pose, then smoothly hit the next pose, and so on. Now the animation should look fairly real.

After the timing is set, you can in-between the poses. The idea here is to hold each pose for a brief period of time, and then make a transition to the next pose. A good rule of thumb is to allow 6–8 frames as a transition (which can change drastically depending on the needs of the shot). The transitions are then set to Bézier curves. From there, it's a matter of tweaking the motion, offsetting frames to get overlap, and so on.

Dope Sheets

A *dope sheet* is a much simpler representation of an animation. A curve is a two-dimensional representation of the motion (a value plotted against time), and a dope sheet boils this down to one dimension. It is simply a line containing marks or dots that denote where the motion changes. In the previous example, when the character starts walking, there's a mark on the dope sheet. When the character stops, there's another mark, and when the character changes direction, there's another mark. This is very much like an animation curve, but without the information about the value of the curve.

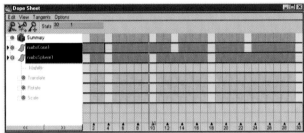

A dope sheet represents keys linearly. In this case (3D Studio MAX), keys are represented as a series of dots.

Depending on the software, a dope sheet can also represent keys as a series of bars. This is how it looks in Maya.

Many times, it's easier to visualize the animation as events in time rather than values. In addition, too many curves on a screen can get confusing. A dope sheet makes it easier to manipulate a large numbers of keyframes. Most dope sheets enable you to select and move dozens of keyframes simultaneously, which is helpful when retiming entire scenes.

Paths/Trajectory

Another way of looking at your animation is through the use of paths. Most packages display the path that your object takes through space. This is a good way of determining exactly how an object is moving. By adjusting the shape and position of the path, you can alter the way an object or character moves through the scene.

Paths are not used that much in character animation, but they can be helpful in places where you need to visualize an action. If you had a character whose arms were manipulated via IK, for example, paths would be a good way to visualize the motion of the arm—which, as you will see later, should move along an arc. Another example might be a character flying through a room. The path indicates the motion of the body in space. In addition to generating a path for keyframed motion, many packages also enable you to draw a spline and use that line as the path. If you want your character to follow a straight line, for example, the path will be straight as well.

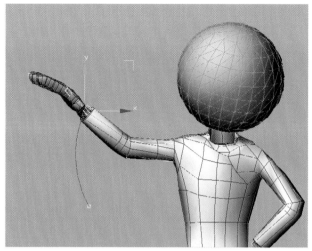

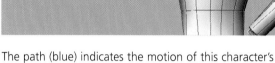

The path (blue) indicates the motion of this character's wrist.

When IK is used, the arm follows the motion of the wrist.

Using Timing to Suggest Weight

Unless your software calculates real-world physics, there is no way to indicate an object's weight. Think of a simple sphere sitting on the ground, as shown in the figure. Is it a bowling ball or a basketball? Until it moves, you have no idea whether the sphere is filled with air or lead. Once the sphere is in motion, however, its characteristics become apparent. A bowling ball is heavy. It moves slowly, and a great deal of force is required to change its direction. A basketball, on the other hand, is relatively light. It moves fast, bounces easily, and it takes very little force to change its direction.

Which sphere is filled with air and which one is filled with lead? Until they move, there is no way of knowing.

Exercise #1: Creating Weight Through Motion

One of the best ways to develop
your sense of timing is to do some
experiments with simple objects,
such as spheres and boxes. These
are great because they can be
modeled and animated fairly
quickly in any 3D package. By
animating simple objects, we also
can focus on pure motion and
timing.

1. Model a sphere, a box, and
    a ground plane. Position the
    sphere and the box on the
    ground plane with some
    distance between them.

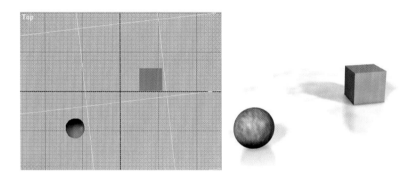

2. Animate the sphere so that it
    travels in a straight line
    toward one face of the box.

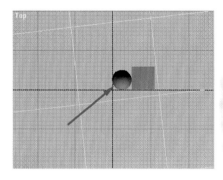

3. When the sphere touches the
    box, change the direction of
    the sphere so that it moves
    off in the opposite direction.
    Keep the box absolutely still.
    Render the shot.

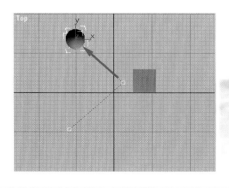

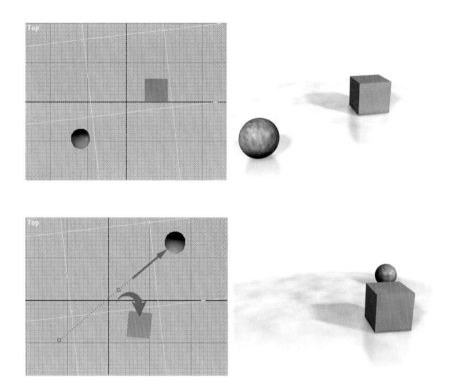

4. This gives us a good example of the box being very heavy, with the ball being relatively light. Let's now reverse the process.

5. Using the same setup as before, animate the sphere so that it travels in a straight line toward the box.

6. This time, when the ball strikes the box, keep the ball moving in a straight line. Next, animate the box by rotating it, as if it were pushed aside by the ball. Render the shot.

7. This gives you a nice example of the ball being much heavier than the box and knocking it out of its path.

What does this example teach us? In both shots, the ball and the box are identical; the only thing that changed is their motion. In the first example, the ball appears light, and in the second, it appears heavy. As you can see, motion and timing affect our perception of an object's weight.

The Language of Movement

The animator must also understand the language of movement. By that, I mean animation has a very specific vocabulary of motion that animators can draw from. This vocabulary includes such things as arcs, anticipation, overshoot, secondary motion, follow-through, overlap, and moving holds, among others. These motions are the raw material; good timing is the glue that holds it all together.

Arcs

In nature, nearly everything moves in arcs. This is partly due to physics and the way muscles move, but it is also due to the fact that nearly every joint in the body rotates. The arm doesn't just move forward; the shoulders and elbow rotate in combination to move the arm, which produces a natural rotation of the hand and fingers as well.

Gravity is another big factor in causing objects to move along arcs. Falling objects and cartoon characters' bodies follow arcs. Gravity causes planets to follow elliptical orbits. It also causes a thrown ball to follow a parabolic trajectory. As you can see, arcs are everywhere in nature.

The rotation of an arm's joints causes the hand to move along an arc.

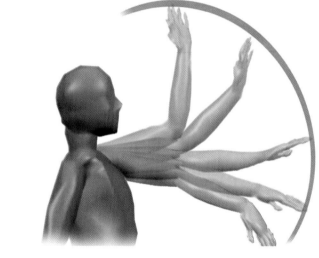

A ball thrown in the air also follows an arc.

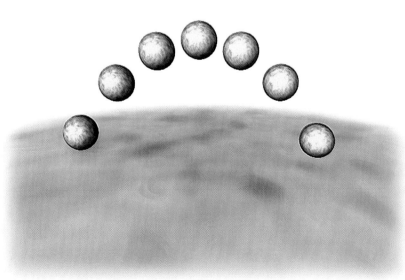

One good example of arcs in action is the simple head turn. Suppose we want to turn our character's head to the left. Our first instinct is to simply rotate it along a horizontal straight line. This makes the head look mechanical. In real life, heads dip slightly below horizontal as they turn, making a shallow arc.

Heads do not turn on straight lines.

Instead, they dip slightly in the middle of the turn, forming an arc.

Slow-Ins and Slow-Outs

Another fact about natural motions is that things don't just start and stop suddenly. Rather, they accelerate from a start and decelerate to a stop. Force plays a role in this. Newtonian physics states that any object subjected to a force will accelerate. Think of a ball thrown straight up. The force of gravity will slow it to a stop and then accelerate the ball as it falls back to Earth. In animation, this effect is known as a *slow-in* and *slow-out*.

Although gravity is certainly one force that acts on your characters, there are plenty of others. Forces can be external—a character being pushed, pulled, or moved by some outside object, for example. Forces can also be internal, coming from inside the character's body—the muscle puts a constant force on the joint, for example, which accelerates the limb in one direction. Another muscle pulls it in the opposite direction, slowing it to a stop. Expanding upon this concept, even a character's internal thoughts and emotions can be thought of as forces—an indecisive character moves much differently than a self-assured one.

When performing a slow-in or slow-out, it's best to use a Bézier curve, which naturally slows in and out. There are many times, however, when you might not want to do a slow-in or slow-out. If a character hits a brick wall, for instance, it stops dead in its tracks, without decelerating. In this case, a linear or step curve might be more appropriate.

As this character is pushed, he slowly accelerates. In animation, this is known as a slow-in.

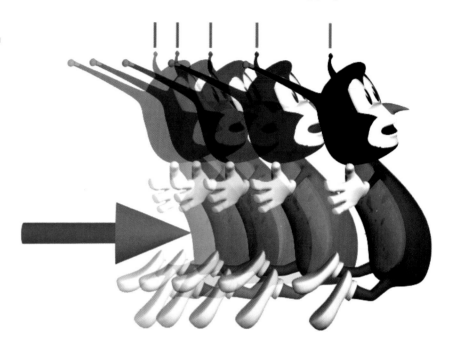

The animation curve for a slow-in and slow-out looks something like this. Notice how the curve slopes toward horizontal as the speed nears zero.

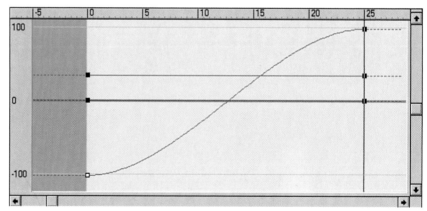

Force and Drag

When animating, you also need to consider the effects of drag on an object. Force transmitted to an object does not affect all parts of the object equally. Imagine two sticks connected through a flexible joint. If you pull one of the sticks straight down, the second stick takes a while to "get in line," so to speak. This effect is called *drag,* and is also known as *lag*.

Drag causes the second joint to take some time to follow the first. If you pull down on the first stick…

…the second stick must rotate to get into alignment with the first.

Drag causes a delay in the two sticks lining up.

Another point to consider is how a multijointed object will move. If an object has more than two joints, each joint drags behind the other. A third stick added to the first two simply drags behind the second.

Three sticks simply means more drag. The third stick drags behind the second, which drags behind the first.

The same principles apply to the joints of your character. The spine is really just a collection of similar joints. Force transmitted to one end of the spine takes time to reach the other end. Force applied to the arm takes time to reach the shoulder and even longer to reach the feet. Think of a dog's tail. The joints in the tail behave exactly like the joints in our stick example. The base of the tail rotates in a cycle, causing the outer parts of the tail to drag.

The body's skeleton is really just a collection of joints. Force applied to one part of the skeleton takes time to reach the others.

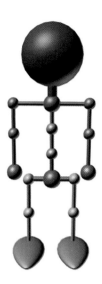

A dog's tail behaves exactly like our sticks. The end of the tail drags behind the base.

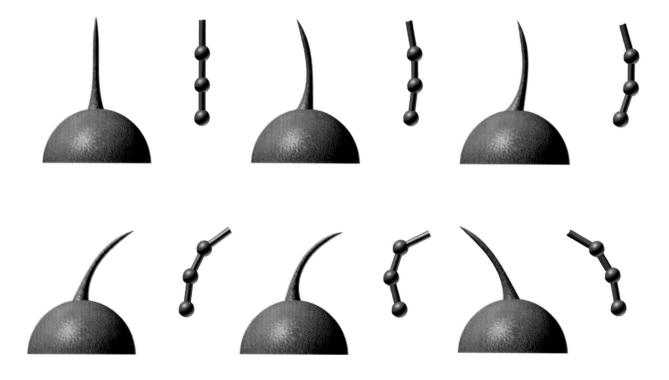

Squash-and-Stretch

Unless you're animating the Statue of Liberty, your characters will usually be made of flesh. Flesh is very pliable and flexes and bends considerably when moving. Think of how many different shapes the human face can make. The same goes for just about any part of the body. This characteristic is known by animators as *squash-and-stretch*.

The easiest way to illustrate this concept is with a bouncing ball. When the ball hits the ground, the force of impact makes it "squash" from a sphere into an oblong shape. As it recoils, you can see it "stretch" in the other direction.

The same principles apply in character animation. When a character jumps in the air, it stretches as it takes off and squashes when it lands. The same goes for things such as muscles and limbs. This does not mean the character has to literally stretch in volume. Realistic animals and humans have squash-and-stretch as well. If a character lands on the ground, the skeleton bends at the knees (squashes) to absorb the shock of impact. If the character leaps off the screen, the knees straighten (stretch) when it flies through the air.

When a ball hits the ground, the force of impact squashes it. Upon recoil, it stretches.

In much the same way, a flour sack also squashes when it hits the ground.

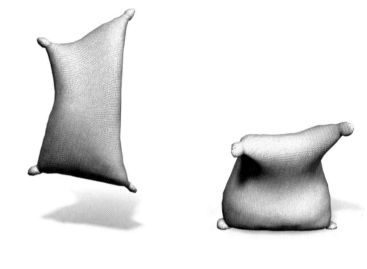

A slightly more complex character squashes in much the same way.

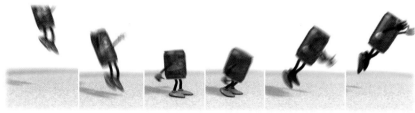

For an exaggerated, cartoonish effect, a character falling down a hole can stretch quite a bit in a few frames.

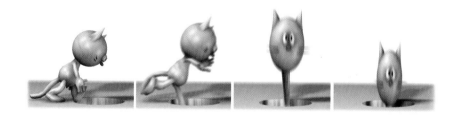

When squashing and stretching, you must remember to maintain your character's volume. Consider a balloon filled with water. If you stretch it or squash it, the water in one part of the balloon simply moves to another area. Never does the volume change. People are mostly water as well, so the same principle applies. No matter how squashed or distended the character, its volume always remains the same. If the volume increases or decreases, it appears as though the character is growing or shrinking.

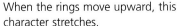

When the rings move upward, this character stretches.

Just making the body longer will not work—the character gains volume and simply looks taller.

Narrowing the chest area (arrows) maintains volume and makes the stretch look natural.

How to Squash and Stretch a Character

Exactly how you squash and stretch a character in a computer depends a great deal on how the character is built and how it is deformed. Let's look at some methods for squashing and stretching your characters.

Proper Posing

Many times, particularly with quasi-realistic characters, you will not want to do a hyper-cartoonish stretch and you will not want to play with the volume of the character. In these cases, the best squash-and-stretch is to simply pose the skeleton properly. When a character squash-es, bend the knees and curve the spine to make the character squash realistically. When the character is stretching, straighten the legs and spine to get a stretch that is anatomically correct.

Squash-and-stretch need not be a cartoonish effect. It is a part of every motion of every creature on the planet. The cartoon character is simply exaggerating this effect for maximum contrast. Even when doing these types of effects, you need to first get the pose of the skeleton correct before manipulating the volume of the character. Exaggeration is always based in reality.

Scaling

The easiest method for squashing and stretching is to simply scale all or part of your character along one axis. If your character is being squashed, reduce its size along the axis; increase it to stretch the character. To maintain volume, however, you also need to increase or reduce the volume along the other two axes accordingly.

Scaling an object along one axis alone increases its volume. You must compensate by scaling back along the other axis.

Skeletal Deformation

If your character has a skeleton, you can get squash-and-stretch fairly easily by manipulating the bones. Most packages that support bones enable you to scale and resize each bone. The affected vertices of your character's mesh will scale accordingly. If you want to stretch the arm, for example, simply scale the bones in the arm. Most of the same principles of scaling apply here as well; if you stretch the bone in one direction, shrink it along the others to maintain volume.

Another way to achieve stretch with a skeleton is to manipulate the space between the bones. This really works only with forward kinematics, but if you want a character to stretch, simply move the bones further apart. A similar technique works for IK systems that are set up using constraints. In the skeleton constructed in Chapter 6, "Skeletons and Mesh Deformation," the foot was constrained to the leg at the ankle. If the foot is moved beyond the length of the leg, the foot will separate from the ankle, causing the same effect as separating the bones (although the effect is localized near the ankle).

Some, but not all, IK systems have features that allow stretch to occur automatically. When the joint hits its limit, such as in the previous example, the skeleton automatically stretches the bones to meet the effector. This means the entire leg stretches to meet the foot.

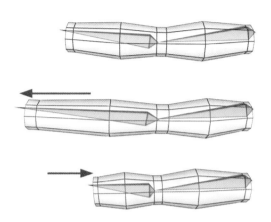

Scaling a bone along its length squashes and stretches a joint.

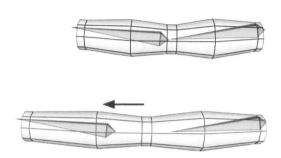

With forward kinematics, you can also stretch by manipulating the distances between the bones.

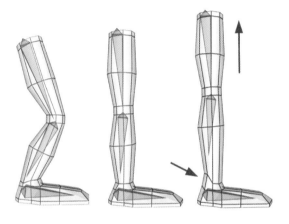

This leg is manipulated via IK with a constraint to the foot. If the leg is pulled past the IK limit, the bones separate at the ankle, which stretches the leg at the ankle.

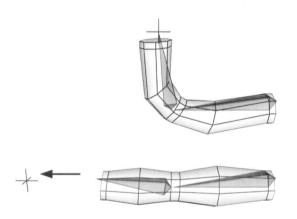

Normally, in most IK systems, when the effector goes beyond the limits of the joints, the bones remain the same length.

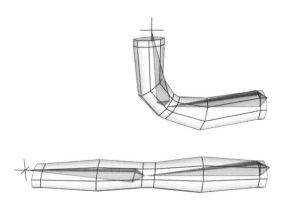

Some systems, however, allow the bones to automatically scale to meet the effector.

Lattices and Other Deformations

Lattice deformations—as well as global deformations that allow you to bend, taper, or otherwise modify the shape of your object—are great for creating squash-and-stretch. You can apply these to the character as a whole or just to part of a character, if your software allows it.

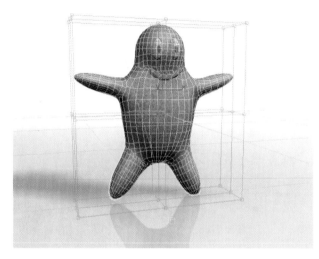 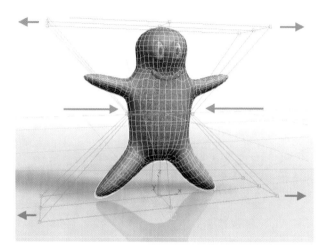

Another way to squash or stretch all or part of a character is with a deformation tool, such as this lattice.

Manipulating the lattice causes the character to stretch.

Automatic Stretching

Another method of squash-and-stretch is to let the computer do the stretching for you. Many packages contain soft body dynamics systems, which can simulate the motion of soft objects, such as skin. This makes it easy to create characters with floppy ears or jiggly bellies. Soft bodies can also be used to create other types of motion, such as overlap and follow-through, two more techniques that are explained a bit later.

Anticipation

Anticipation is also the body's natural way of gaining momentum before an action begins. Think of a man jumping. He swings his arms behind him, bends his knees, and actually moves down slightly to get momentum before jumping up. A baseball batter moves the bat back before swinging it forward. A character leans back before getting out of a chair. It's sort of like getting a head start on the action.

Anticipation can also be used to control the audience and get your viewers to look exactly where you want them to. The human eye works somewhat automatically. It is naturally drawn to things that move. By moving an object in the opposite direction, you draw attention to it before it moves. When it does move, the audience is already watching, so the motion can be much faster. Anticipation is a perfectly natural part of motion, and by exaggerating this, you can keep the audience's attention and achieve crisper timing.

Many times, you may need to animate a very fast action, such as a zip-out, where a character suddenly dashes offscreen. The most important point to remember is that when you animate a fast action, your audience needs to be fully aware of the action before it occurs. This makes anticipation of the action very important.

Never underestimate the importance of anticipating your character's motions when you are animating simply because it's the way the body naturally moves. An anticipation does not have to be a big motion or a giant pause in the action. It can be as short and subtle as a few frames for a small action.

Anticipation means moving left before you move right and moving down before moving up. Before this character zips off, she cocks her body in anticipation of the move.

Before this character puts his hand in the hat, he anticipates the move by flipping his wrist back before moving it down.

Exercise #2: Anticipation

Simply by making a character leap out of frame, you can see how anticipation works. Before you do this exercise, stand up and do a small jump. Pay attention to how your knees bend and your arms anticipate the jump by moving back before swinging forward when you jump. If you want to, use a stopwatch as you jump to get a rough idea of the timing.

1. Place your character in the shot in a simple, relaxed pose.

2. Rotate the arms back and bend the knees in anticipation of the leap. To maintain balance, the body should tilt forward and down at the hips. This anticipation should take about 1/4–1/2 second past the first pose.

3. Make your character leap. Straighten the body and swing the arms forward. Straighten the legs as they push against the ground and send the character forward. This action should take only a few frames to complete.

4. Render a test and adjust the poses and timing until you are satisfied.

This simple leap can be expanded with other little details. First, when leaping, the arms lead the action by a frame or two. The feet do not have to leave the ground at the same time; dragging one foot by a frame or two behind the other may make the leap more natural as well. Finally, remember that the path your character will follow is the beginning of a parabola. As the character leaps out, make it follow an arc.

Overshoot

As we've seen, anticipation is used to make the start of an action more lifelike. At the tail end of the action, you have overshoot. Many times, the body will not come to a slow and perfect stop. Instead, it will overshoot the stopping point for a few frames and settle into the pose. Like anticipation, it is a natural part of motion and can be exaggerated to the animator's advantage.

Think of a character throwing out its arm to point a finger. Before the action starts, the arm anticipates the move. If the motion is quick, the character's arm naturally overshoots the pose so that the arm is absolutely straight. It may even stretch past this point for an even more exaggerated effect. After a few frames, the arm settles into a more natural, relaxed pose. Overshoot can be used to give your character's actions more snap. If you're animating pose-to-pose, you can overshoot a pose for a few frames and then settle in.

When this character throws out his arm, he overshoots the final pose for a few frames and settles in.

Secondary Action

We've been concentrating on the primary motions of the body; many parts of the body move also. This is known to animators as *secondary action*. This broad category of actions includes the little tweaks, gestures, and touches that add extra life and personality to your character. It could be as simple as a character tilting his hat before storming off, or a baby in a high chair wiggling her toes while she eats. The primary action is eating, but the secondary action—tilting the hat, wiggling the toes—adds personality and life to the character as a whole.

Secondary action is best animated as a layer on the primary action. First, animate the main motion. When this is correct, add the secondary actions. They should be little extra touches and not detract from the main point of the shot. Secondary actions are usually bracketed around the main action, but they do not interfere. Remember, the cardinal rule in animation is to do one thing at a time. The secondary actions serve as a nice, subtle bridge between the main actions. If they get too wild or noticeable, they become primary actions themselves and detract from the shot.

Another angle to this is the psychological gesture. If a character is talking and keeps brushing at his nose, the character is giving away a psychological place of interest. Perhaps the character really needs to sneeze. Another example might be a character looking at his watch while he walks. This secondary action has now become a psychological gesture explaining that the character is in a hurry.

Many people use the term "secondary motion" to describe any action outside the main action, such as the motion of hair or clothing. Although this has become standard lingo for many animators, technically, many of these types of action fall under the subcategory of overlap and follow-through.

Overlap and Follow-Through

When a character comes to a stop, not every part of its body stops on the same frame. Momentum carries some parts of the body past the stopping point. When parts of the body still move after a character has come to a stop, that movement is called follow-through. As part of secondary motion, follow-through motions are driven more by the laws of physics rather than the internal motivations of the character.

Think of a dog with big, floppy ears. After the dog has stopped walking, its ears continue to move, much like a pendulum. Drag also plays a big part in this. Overlap is almost identical to follow-through, because it involves secondary motion of the body. The body itself has many parts that don't all move at once—a fat person's belly bounces up and down during a walk, overlapping the action by several frames, for example. As with squash-and-stretch, these effects can be achieved through a soft-body dynamics module.

Follow-through also applies to the limbs of a body. The hips usually start an action, with the spine and arms dragging by a few frames. Think of an athlete completing a broad jump. His feet may hit the ground, but it may take many frames for the arms to swing forward and come to a complete stop. Again, they act a bit like a pendulum.

The dog doesn't stop all at once.

His front feet stop first...

…then his ears, collar, and tail follow through…   …and come to rest a few frames later.

It's also important to have overlap in the actions of the scene as a whole. Things do not move all at once. Think of the situation where many characters are walking through the scene. If you start all the walks on frame 1, they appear to march in unison. Instead, the best choice is to overlap the motions of the walk, offsetting some of the characters.

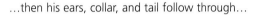

Exercise #3: Using Overshoot, Overlap, and Follow-Through

Let's make that other half of the leap you just created by making your character land. This shows you how different parts of the body follow through, overlap, and overshoot poses as a character moves.

Again, before animating this shot, act out the action. Stand up and take a short hop. Notice how, as you land, your knees bend to absorb the shock and your arms naturally swing forward.

1. The character should come in from the leap in a few frames. As the character is about to land, his knees should be slightly bent, his hips forward, and his arms and shoulders back.

2. Two frames later, the character touches ground. The feet hit heel-first, stop, and lock to the ground. The rest of the body, though, is nowhere near stopping.

3. Two frames later, the momentum of the body is still downward and forward, forcing the knees to bend and the body to bend forward at the waist to absorb the shock. The arms are still back.

4. Three frames later, the body has now recoiled and is beginning to stand up. The spine is straightening out, one vertebra at a time due to drag, and the knees are straightening. The arms swing forward and start following through.

5. Four frames later, the body is overshooting the final pose. The spine and legs are almost straight, and the arms are coming to a stop above the head and beginning to move back down again.

6. Six frames later is the final pose. The spine and legs bend a bit for a nice relaxed stance. The arms hang loose.

7. Render a test and adjust the poses and timing until you are happy with the shot.

For additional practice, you can hook up this landing with the leap from the previous exercise. When doing this, remember that your character's center of mass will follow a smooth parabola during the leap.

Cycles

One way to save time when doing animation is to animate in cycles. A cycle is simply the same sequence of keyframes repeated. Think of somebody riding a bicycle. The feet on the pedals undergo a regular, cyclical motion. After you've animated one rotation of the pedals, you can simply copy the keys to create as many repetitions as you want.

Riding a bicycle is a good example of the repetitive motions that can be handled by cycles.

In cel animation, the process is simply a matter of repeating your drawings. In 3D animation, you copy the keyframes to other places on the time line. One problem with doing this is you need to remember that the last keys of the first cycle need to flow into the first key of the next. Many programs have a function that aligns your keys automatically for a smooth transition and repeats the cycle for as many times as you want. If you don't have such features, the best way to do this is manually. You simply copy the first frame of the first cycle to the first frame of the next cycle before you begin animating. That way, you always have a target so you can see that the last few frames of the cycle match up with the next.

Another problem with cycles is that they are repetitive motions, and as such, can get stale and boring very quickly. You can avoid this by cycling only part of a character's motions. Let's say the character is walking. You can cycle the feet and legs, but change the animation in the upper body to give the shot more variation.

Moving Holds

There are many times where your character may need to hold a pose or be still—from a few frames to a few seconds. This is known as a *hold*. In cel animation, this is typically done by simply holding a single drawing on the screen for the duration of the hold. In computer animation, this can be very problematic. For some unexplained reason—maybe because of the realistic nature of the medium—a digital character held in a single position for more than a few frames will completely die. It looks as though you hit the freeze-frame button on the VCR.

A character left immobile on the screen looks as if you hit the freeze-frame button.

Move the character slightly over the duration of the hold. Here, the character has shifted his weight to his right slightly. Be sure to overlap these motions.

In order to get around this, you always keep your character moving, even slightly. There are any number of tricks for doing this. One is to create moving holds. If the hold is for a handful of frames, you can simply create two slightly different variations of the same pose and have the computer in-between these over the course of the hold.

If the hold is in the range of seconds, you have to use another method. Secondary actions help a lot, but you should overlap many subtle actions in the hold to keep the character from looking too mechanical.

You may want to shift the character's weight from one foot to another. Move the arm slightly. Tilt the head. Add some blinks. If you have the ability to animate your character's chest, make it breathe. Be sure to overlap these subtle motions as well. It's really a matter of keeping the character still, but still alive.

A good exercise is to stand in the corner for a minute or two and try to remain still. If you pay attention to your body, you'll soon realize that it's constantly moving. Your weight may shift from foot to foot, you're constantly breathing, you're blinking, and so forth. These are the same actions you can use to keep your character looking alive.

You should also remember environmental things, such as wind, temperature, gravity, and so on. If the character is holding its arm out, gravity will affect it. Let the arm droop slightly over time. If your character has hair, a slight breeze might help bring the hair to life. If it's cold outside, the character may shiver.

Putting It All Together

These last two exercises use most of the techniques you've learned so far. Use them as a way to develop and hone your skills.

Exercise #4: Standing Up

By making a character stand up from a seated position, you use anticipation, drag, overlap, follow-through, and overshoot, among other techniques.

Before you go any further, you should get up from your chair several times. Notice exactly how your body moves. You lean back

to anticipate the move, and then you lean forward and stand up. This gives you a guideline for the motion, but what about the timing? If you have a stopwatch, time yourself standing up and use that to block in your timing; otherwise, use the timing I give you and adjust it to your needs.

Load a character into your 3D program. Next, model a simple box for the character to sit on. If you want to create a chair or a sofa for the character to sit on, that's fine, but not essential.

1. Seat your character in a relaxed position. This is your first pose.

2. For your character to stand up, it needs to anticipate the move to help it get some momentum. Rotate the upper body back at the hips. As in the jump exercise, the arms should go back slightly as well. This is your second pose. Place this keyframe approximately 1/4–1/2 second after the first.

3. As the body gets out of the chair, it leans forward quite a bit, with the momentum of the upper body pulling the rear end out of the chair as the weight is transferred to the feet. Rotate the upper body forward, and rotate the knees so that the rear end is slightly out of the chair. Also, swing the arms forward to help maintain balance, but drag them behind the body by a few frames. Again, 1/4–1/2 second is a good general timing.

4. Create a standing pose. Remember to keep the feet firmly on the ground as the character stands, either by locking them in place with IK or by watching and manipulating the keys carefully. This timing should take anywhere from 1/2 second to 1 second after the previous key. The arms also do a bit of follow-through and come to a stop a few frames after the body is standing.

5. Let the computer calculate the in-betweens. If your computer is fast enough, press Play; otherwise, render a test to see how you did. Go back and rework the timing and poses until you are happy with the shot.

Exercise #5: Animating a Flour Sack

This last simple exercise makes a flour sack jump off a box and land. Animate this shot pose-to-pose by blocking out each of the major parts of the shot. Then, time the poses to get a good sense of weight. Finally, let the system in-between the poses and tweak from there.

1. Create a simple set containing a box and a floor plane.

2. Place your flour sack in the set. Give the flour sack a natural starting pose. Asymmetrical poses are best.

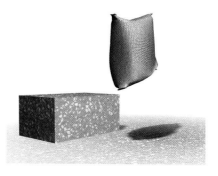

3. To make the sack jump, it needs to get its weight into it. This is done by bending the character at the waist and anticipating the jump. This should take about 6–8 frames.

4. Create the take-off position. Stretch the sack upward while keeping the feet planted. This should take 4–6 frames.

5. Pose the top of the leap. The sack will not be stretched at the top of the leap. Remember slow-in and slow-out, which tells us the flour sack moves along a parabola. The feet also rotate forward a bit in preparation for landing. This should take 8–12 frames.

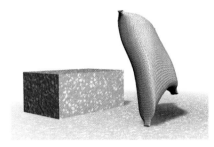

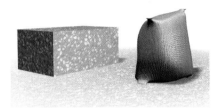

6. Pose the landing. As the character falls back to the ground, gravity stretches the lower part of the sack. Typically, both feet won't hit the ground at once, so keep this pose asymmetrical. This should take 8–12 frames.

7. As the flour sack's weight hits the ground, it will squash, perhaps bending over a bit as well. Squash it anywhere from 4–8 frames.

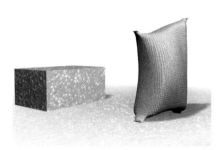

8. The sack finally stands up in a stable pose. It may need to take a step to get into this pose. After the poses are blocked out, play with the timing to get the best sense of weight. Standing up should take 6–12 frames.

9. After these major poses are set, tweak the timing to get overlap and follow-through. The timing given here is very rough. Learn to derive the timing yourself so that you understand what feels right and what doesn't.

Conclusion

In this chapter, you explored the basic animation concepts, such as squash-and-stretch, anticipation, and secondary motion. These techniques are the palette of motion and the colors with which you bring your characters to life. These techniques tell you why and where to place the keyframes in an animation. The chapter also presented the basics of most 3D packages and how they relate to these concepts, which showed you how to set and manipulate the keyframes. Understanding these tools helps you control your characters and their motions better.

CHAPTER 9

Walking and Locomotion

Now that you've had a bit of practice with animating the human figure, it's time to start moving your characters around. By moving, I mean walking and running. Walking requires tons of balance and coordination; it's amazing how easy people make it look.

Walking conveys a great deal about a character's personality. The next time you're in a crowded place, notice all the different types of walks that people have. Some people waddle, others saunter, and some drag their feet. It's amazing how almost everyone you see has a unique walk. Mae West, Groucho Marx, John Wayne, and Charlie Chaplin are all characters who have very distinctive walks. If you want to know who a character is, figure out how he walks.

Computer animators have a number of tools available for animating walks. It seems as though software vendors have focused on this problem with considerable effort, and quite a few new and innovative tools are available for automating all or part of the walking process. These sophisticated tools can be both good and bad. As the animator, you should still understand exactly how characters walk and how you want your characters to walk. If a piece of software enables you to get this done in half the time, that's fantastic. Just be sure that you are the one controlling the process, not a piece of software. If the computer does the animation, it will look computerized—stale, mechanical, and lifeless.

Understanding the Mechanics of Walking

Walking has been described as "controlled falling." Every time you take a step, you actually lean forward and fall slightly, and are caught by your outstretched foot. If you failed to put your foot forward, you would fall flat on your face. After your foot touches the ground, your body's weight is transferred to it and your knee bends to absorb the shock. The front leg then lifts the body and propels it forward as the rear leg swings up to catch you again, and the cycle repeats.

Before you read any further, get up and walk around the room for a bit. Pay attention to how each part of your body moves. You'll soon notice that every part of the body, from the feet to the arms to the head, has its own unique set of motions. As you walk around, notice how you lean forward into the walk, and how your legs neatly catch your body to prevent it from falling. If you purposely hold your foot back on a step, you'll fall flat on your face.

The process of walking is very complex. Not only do the feet have to move across the ground, but the hips, spine, arms, shoulders, and head all move in sync to keep the system in balance. Although these movements are complex, if you break them down joint by joint, the mechanics of walking becomes clear.

The following sections break down a basic walk, step by step. For clarity, I've animated a simple skeleton so you can see how each joint moves.

Feet and Legs

The feet and legs propel the body forward. To keep your character looking natural, you should always keep the joints bent slightly, even at full leg extension.

On the CD

On the CD are four animations that show you this walk from four different views. These files are called WALK1.AVI through WALK4.AVI (Mac users should load WALK1.MOV through WALK4.MOV). Watch these animations for reference.

The walk usually starts with the feet at the extended position, where the feet are farthest apart and where the character's weight shifts to the forward foot.

As the weight of the body is transferred to the forward foot, the forward knee bends to absorb the shock. This position is called the recoil position, and is the lowest point in the walk.

This figure illustrates the point halfway through the first step. As the character moves forward, the forward knee straightens out and lifts the body to its highest point. This position is called the passing position because the free foot passes the supporting leg at this point.

As the character moves forward, the weight-bearing foot lifts off the ground at the heel, transmitting the force to the ball of the foot. The body starts to fall forward. The free foot swings forward like a pendulum to meet the ground and catch the body's weight.

The free leg makes contact with the ground, completing half the cycle. The second half is an exact mirror of the first. If it differs, the character may appear to limp.

The Hips, Spine, and Shoulders

The body's center of gravity is at the hips; all balance starts there, as does the rest of the body's motion. During a walk, it's best to think of the hips' motion as two separate, overlapping rotations. First, the hips rotate along the axis of the spine, forward and back with the legs. If the right leg is forward, the right hip is rotated forward. Second, at the passing position, the free leg pulls the hip out of center, forcing the hips to rock from side to side. These two motions are then transmitted through the spine to the shoulders, which mirror the hips to maintain balance.

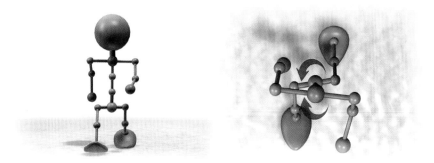

When the feet are fully extended, the hips must rotate along the axis of the spine. To keep balance, the shoulders swing in the opposite direction. From the front, the spine is relatively straight, but from the top, you can see how the hips and shoulders twist in opposite directions to maintain balance.

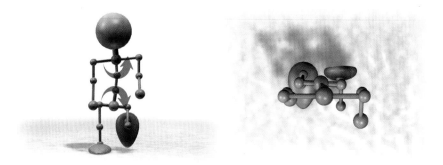

At the passing position, the front view shows the hip being pulled out of center by the weight of the free leg, causing a counter-rotation in the shoulders. From the top, the hips and shoulders are at nearly equal angles. The hip also moves slightly off center, moving away from the free leg. If all the weight of the character is evenly distributed in the center all the time, the walk looks static and dead.

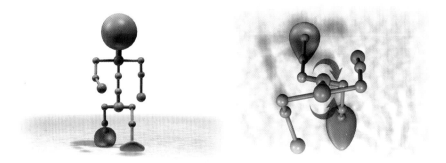

At the extension of the second leg, the hips and shoulders again are flat when viewed from the front. From the top, you can see the completed rotation of the hips and shoulders.

The Arms

Unless the character is holding something or gesturing, its arms generally hang loose at the sides. When walking, they act like a pendulum, dragging a few frames behind the motion of the hips and shoulders. Even at full extension, the arms should be slightly bent at the elbows to keep them looking natural.

The Head and Spine from the Side

If you look at a character's spine from the side, you can see its general posture, which may be very stiff or slouched over, depending on the character's attitude. The spine also absorbs some of the shock transmitted to the hips from the legs, making it flex from front to back a bit.

In a standard walk, the head tries to stay level, with the eyes pointing in the direction of the walk, but it bobs around slightly to stay balanced. If a character is excited, this bobbing is more pronounced. The head may also hang low for a sad character, or may look around if the scene requires it.

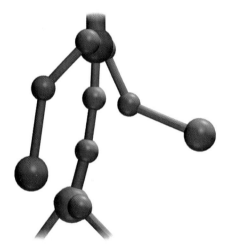

Because walking is kind of like falling forward, the body should be angled forward slightly at the hips for most walks. The spine arches up slightly to keep the chest and head over the hips. However, this line of action can change with the character's attitude.

For example, if a character is terribly sad, he tends to hunch forward and hang his head low. This posture forces the hips to rotate in the opposite direction, giving the body a different attitude. He'll most likely drag his feet as well.

Animating a Walk

Now that you understand the underlying mechanics of walking, you can attempt to animate a walk. Using traditional animation techniques, a walk cycle is tough; it can be just as tricky on a computer.

Timing the Walk

The first thing you need to concern yourself with is the timing of the walk. How many frames does it take? That's not an easy question to answer. Is your character large and lumbering or small and scrappy? Is your character running or walking? Happy or sad? All these factors determine the amount of time it takes your character to take a step.

At a normal walking gait, a step takes anywhere from 1/3–2/3 second (8–16 frames at 24fps, or 10–20 frames at 30fps) with 1/2 second per step being about average. A full cycle (both right and left steps) takes about 1 second per cycle. Larger characters tend to walk slower, and smaller characters walk faster. In general, men have slightly slower gaits than women, and sad people walk slower than happy people.

One nice thing about working with a computer is that many programs enable you to scale the length of your animation. If your character is walking too slowly, you can speed it up a bit by reworking the keys.

Keeping Your Feet on the Ground

The most important thing to remember when animating a walk is to keep your character's feet firmly locked to the ground. The friction between the feet and the ground propels the character forward. If the feet slide around, the illusion of friction is lost and the animation will not seem realistic. (If your character is walking on banana peels or an oil slick, sliding may seem hilarious.)

How do you keep the feet locked to the ground? It really depends on your software and its feature set. Many packages have tools to assist you in this task; others do not. The following are a few of the more popular methods:

- Inverse kinematics (IK) with constraints—IK is one of the preferred walk-animation methods because it ensures that a character's grounded foot stays in the same spot for the duration of the step. Knowing that the feet are locked frees the animator's mind from annoying details and enables him to concentrate on more important things, such as posing the character.

■ Footstep generators—Some packages have what I call "footstep generators." These plug-ins enable you to toss down footprints on the ground, up hills, down ladders, wherever you want. The program then automatically moves the character's legs and feet to match. Typically, the motion is generated by an algorithm that computes the character's physical weight and dynamics.

Using such a plug-in is a great way to get the first pass of a walk into the computer, but that's about it. One bad thing about this type of automation is that the walk is typically generated from the feet and not the hips. Animators must keep this in mind when tweaking the animation, because most all movement in a walk leads from the hips. As the animator, you still need to control the process and add personality to the walk. You must go back over the animation and tweak the poses and motion on a second and third pass to add the flavor and individuality that makes your character unique.

■ Inverse or broken hierarchies—This method does not require IK and works with any package that supports forward kinematics. In a normal skeleton, the hips are at the top of the tree, with the spine and legs as children. If you don't have a way to lock the feet, this setup can cause problems, because moving the hips moves the spine, legs, and feet.

In the inverse hierarchy method, the hierarchy is turned upside down and broken at the hips. The feet become the parents of the legs, enabling you to place the feet where you want them. Because they're the parents, you can rest assured that they won't move unless you absolutely want them to move.

What about the hips? In a hierarchy, because an object can't have two parents, the hips must be disconnected from the legs and are forced to float free above them. The hips are then animated to match up with the legs. Because exactly matching the hips to the legs can be problematic, this method works best for characters whose hips are hidden—a soda can with feet or a character in a skirt. It also works well when using bones, because the character's skin tends to obscure most hip-alignment problems. Besides, viewers usually notice the feet slipping long before they notice that the hips are not quite connected; it's the lesser of two evils.

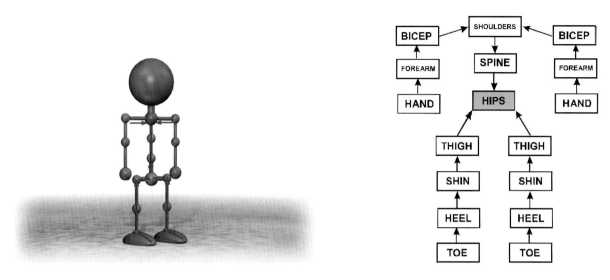

In a normal hierarchy, all joints point to the hips. Thus, by moving the hips, you move the entire body. This method can make it very easy for the feet to slip inadvertently.

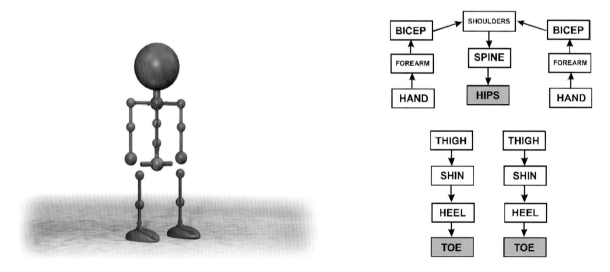

In an inverse hierarchy, the link is broken at the hips, and the feet become parents of the legs. The feet never move unless you tell them to, and they never slip.

■ Forward kinematics with guides—If, for some reason, none of these other methods works, you can tough it out and keyframe the walk by hand. To aid in this process, you can always use guides to aid in the placement of the feet. In any package, you can place null objects, dummies, or transparent objects along the character's feet and use them as virtual placeholders. If the foot moves inadvertently, you have a reference point that enables you to put the foot back where it belongs.

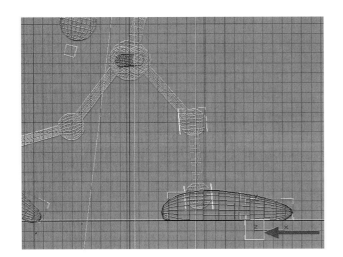
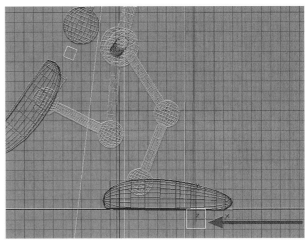

This box is being used as a guide in the placement of the foot. By aligning a reference point on the foot to the guide, you can be reasonably sure it won't slip.

Some packages enable you to simulate an "onionskin" effect by ghosting the previous frame, providing a good simulation of the traditional animator's light table. Because you can see where the feet are on the previous frames, it's rather easy to align them on the current frame.

Finally, some animators have been known to use dry-erase pens to draw the guides directly on the computer screen. The marks can then be erased simply by wiping them off. Still, I'd hate for you to grab the wrong pen and make permanent marks on the screen, so be careful! A good substitute might be a sticky note placed on the screen and marked with a pencil.

To Cycle or Not to Cycle?

Because walking is a cyclical motion, you may want to create the walking motion as a cycle rather than as straight-ahead animation. If done properly, a cycle can save a lot of animation time. One cycle can be applied to a number of different environments. Your character and its cycle can just as easily be placed in a cityscape as a country road, because the walk motion is essentially the same. Why duplicate your efforts? Classical animators use this trick a lot, simply repeating the same sequence of drawings and swapping only the background painting—placing the character in a different location. In 3D, you have the flexibility to change the cameras, lighting, and environment to make the shot look completely different.

Many times, one cycle will look completely different from a different camera angle. This can work for and against you. If you are working on a game animation and the character has an identifiable walk, it must be similar enough to recognize from any camera angles. If you are working on a crowd scene, many times you can use the same walk from a different angle and it looks like a different character walking.

Those who work in the interactive and gaming industries deal with cycles every day. Most game engines require that you animate your characters in cycles, which are then called up as the player uses the joystick. In these cases, you may also need little 3–6 frame animations called links to bridge the gap between cycles—a walk and a run, for example.

There are downsides to using cycles. First, because the cycle is repetitive, it can seem sterile and flat, particularly when viewed for an extended period of time. Second, cycles work best on level terrain. If your character has to walk around a corner or over a hill, the cycle might not match up properly.

Animating a cycle is similar to making your character walk on a treadmill. The body does not move forward; the feet simply move beneath it. To maintain the illusion of walking, the entire character must be moved across the ground (or the ground moved past the character) at the same rate that the feet are moving. Otherwise, the character's feet appear to slip. Also, the foot on the ground needs to move the same distance on each frame. Again, if the length of the steps varies, the feet appear to slip.

This multiple exposure of a walk cycle shows that the body does not move forward; instead, the feet move beneath it. The red marks show how the foot on the ground moves the same distance on each frame to prevent slipping.

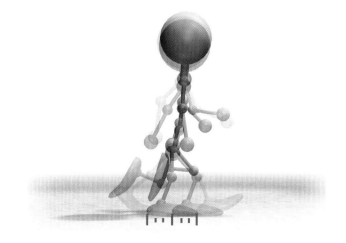

Exercise #1: Walking a Flour Sack

Although it doesn't really have legs or arms, the basic flour sack is a great place to begin when animating a walk. If, as in Chapter 7, "Posing Characters," you picture the sack as the hips and shoulders of a character, you will understand how these parts of the body move when walking.

How you animate the sack depends a bit on how it is deformed. The basic way to deform a sack is simply by placing four bones, one at each corner of the sack, with a fifth bone at the center. Because this structure is so simple, you should not need to link the bones in a hierarchy. Not having them linked also avoids foot placement and slippage problems.

This walk will be timed at 12 frames per step, 24 for the whole cycle.

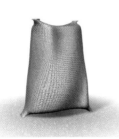

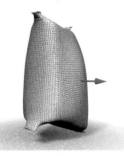

1. Start with the feet slightly apart. Place the left foot forward and the right foot back. To keep the character's weight balanced, make the shoulders mirror the legs. Place the right shoulder forward and the left shoulder back. Set keys for both the shoulders and the feet.

2. Move to frame 6, halfway through the first step. Move the right foot up and forward so that it is even with the left. Set a key.

3. Make sure the bone in the center of the body also moves along. Move it forward so that the weight is centered and set a key.

continues

Exercise: continued

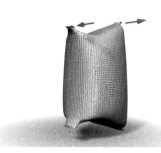

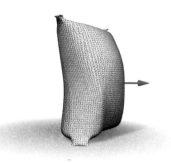

4. Balance out the upper body. Recall how the shoulders mirror the hips in a walk. Move the right shoulder down and back. Move the left shoulder up and forward. Set keys for both.

5. Get the end of the step (and the start of the next). Move the right foot forward and place it firmly on the ground. Set keys for both feet.

6. Move the center bone forward to keep the weight centered between the two feet. Set a key.

7. Mirror the shoulders to the hips by moving the right shoulder up and back. Move the left shoulder down and forward. Set keys for both.

This finishes off the first step. Repeat the procedure for the next foot to get a full cycle, and then again for as many steps as the character needs to take.

To add a bit more life to the walk, you may want to give the sack's belly a bit of bounce. Remember the concepts of drag, overlap, and follow-through. As the sack walks, its belly (controlled by the center bone) tends to drag behind the action a bit. Gravity also tends to pull it toward the ground. Go back over the walk and add a bit of up-and-down motion to the center bone. As the right foot is moving up, for instance, the bone drags behind by 2 or 3 frames, so it doesn't move up until slightly later. If you did the walk properly, you'll see how even a very simple character can be made to walk. Remember this lesson as we move on to more complex characters.

Exercise #2: Animating a Walk Cycle Using Forward Kinematics

In this exercise, you animate a walk cycle without the aid of inverse kinematics or locks. Many animators consider this method to be the long way around, but it's kind of a fail-safe technique; it should work just about anywhere with almost all packages.

This cycle is timed at 16 frames per step, 32 for the whole cycle. You're doing this example with a simple skeleton, but the techniques should transfer well to any two-legged character. The ability to lock your character's feet to the ground is important, but not necessary, as I'll explain along the way.

To begin, load up your character and hierarchical skeleton in your favorite 3D animation program. Create an animation that's 33 frames long. I've added the extra frame to the end as a target for frames in the second half of the cycle. It will not be rendered.

Start by animating the hips and shoulders. It's best to start here, because all other motions derive from the hips. The hips have two separate, overlapping rotations that are mirrored by the shoulders. The first rotation is along the vertical axis of the spine and follows the position of the legs and feet.

On the CD

If you don't have a character, you can always use one from the CD. On the CD is a character named TINKRBOY.DXF or TINKRBOY.3DS; you can use either if you want.

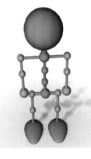

1. Start the walk with the right foot; the right hip must go forward, as well. On frame 1 of the animation, rotate the hips around the y axis so that the right side is forward. From the top view, rotate the shoulders to mirror the hips' rotation.

2. Go to the halfway point (frame 17) in the cycle and rotate the hips and shoulders in the opposite direction. Remember, they should still be mirroring each other. At this point, the hips should also move sideways slightly to maintain balance over the planted foot.

3. Go to 1 frame past the end of the cycle (frame 33) and copy the first frame's keys here. This frame is a target for the frames that are in-betweened on the second half of the cycle.

continues

Exercise: continued

4. Next, you need to create the sway of the hips. Go to the frame in the middle of the first step (frame 9). If your rotations are correct, the hips and shoulders should be parallel when viewed from the top.

    At this point, the passing position or the point of highest leg extension, the body rests on the right leg and the left leg pulls the hips out of center.

5. From the front view, rotate the hips around the z axis so that the right hip is higher. Adjust the spine and shoulders so you get a smooth line of action and the shoulders mirror the hips.

6. Go to the middle frame of the second step (frame 25) and reverse the rotations that you just made at the middle of the first step. The body rests on the left leg at this point, and the spine curves in the opposite direction. Again, the hips move slightly to the left to balance over the planted foot.

7. Adjust the spine on frames 1 and 25 to give it a forward lean and a nice curve.

8. Go back to each keyframe and adjust the legs and arms so that they hang vertically throughout the cycle.

9. Play back the cycle. If it looks smooth and balanced, move on to the next step. Otherwise, tweak the keyframes until you have a nice smooth motion.

10. You now need to move the legs and feet—the trickiest part of the process. First, set up the extreme poses. From a side view, go to frame 1 and set the first pose, where the legs are at maximum extension. Copy these keys to the end of the cycle, at frame 33.

11. Go to the middle of the cycle (frame 17) and mirror frame 1 so that the left leg is forward. A ghosting feature would help considerably in this process.

    To aid in the animation process, use a guide to help position the feet. If you are using locks, you probably won't have to do this step; if you in-between the foot linearly at the two extremes (with no slow-ins or slow-outs), the foot moves across the floor automatically. Still, a guide acts as a nice double-check.

12. To create the guide, model a box and place it directly beneath the floor near the character's forward foot. If it's below the floor, it won't show up at rendering time. You could use a null object.

13. Go to frame 1 and move the guide horizontally to the place where the toe hits the ground.

14. Go to the middle of the cycle (frame 17) and position the guide at the same place on the toe as you did in frame 1.

15. Set up the guide so that it in-betweens these two positions at a linear rate. The guide will tell you exactly where the toe needs to be at any point in the step. (If you have an IK system, you can pin the foot to the guide for a surefire solution.)

continues

Exercise: continued

16. Now, you need to tweak the poses. Because you know where the feet need to be, you can concentrate on the legs. About a quarter of the way through the first step (frame 5) is the recoil position—where the leg absorbs the shock and bends to its lowest point. Move the hips down so that the shin is forced to rotate forward a bit, giving the knee a nice bend.

17. The body recoils upward into the passing position at frame 9. Move the hips up so that the forward leg is fairly well extended. It's very important to keep the knee bent slightly to make the action look natural.

18. At this point, the weight of the body is on the ball of the foot. The heel lifts off the floor as the body falls forward. The hips are moving down at this point. There may also be problems with the free foot as it swings forward; if you have extra-big shoes, they'll hit the floor unless you bend the toes slightly.

19. The first step is now complete. Create a second guide and repeat these procedures for the left foot on the second half of the cycle. Be careful to make the second half as close to the first as possible. Render a test and go back to tweak any inconsistencies.

Now you need to create the motion of the arms and head. In the simplest case, the arms swing back and forth to maintain balance in opposition to the legs. The arms also drag behind the action a bit, placing the arms' extreme poses a few frames behind the legs.

20. Rotate the arms into position on the first frame. Because the right leg is forward, the right arm is back, and the left arm is forward.

21. Go a few frames (from 2–5) in for the arm's extreme pose. I chose frame 5. On the left arm, rotate the forearm back to a nice extension. On the right, rotate the forearm up slightly.

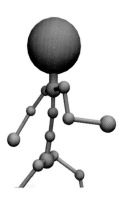

22. Go a few frames (from 2–5) past the start of the second step and mirror the extreme from the previous step. Finally, copy the keys on frame 1 to the last frame so the arm will swing through to the end of the cycle.

23. Now you need to do the head. Go to the keys at the start and halfway through each step and rotate the head so that it remains vertical and the eyes are facing forward. The head can bob from side to side a bit, as long as it's not too distracting.

24. You can also make the spine bounce up and down a bit. Remember the effects of drag that you learned in Chapter 8, "Basics of Character Animation." This applies to the spine as well. If you want, you can make the spine flex between curved and straight, dragging behind the up-and-down motion of the hips by a few frames. As the hips go up, the spine compresses into a curve. When the hips come down again, drag causes the spine to straighten out.

Now that you have a convincing cycle, you need to get your character off the treadmill and out into the world. To do this, you can do one of two things: Either move the character along the ground or move the ground under the character. Moving the ground is best when you want to use a panning camera that is locked on the character; because the character is still, the camera can remain still. Moving the character is best in cases when you want the camera stable and the character to walk past.

In this example, move the ground. If you used a guide to assist in your animation, the task is simple. Find the absolute position of your first guide in frame 1, and then again when it stops in the middle of the cycle.

For example, in my shot, the guide moves along the x axis. The first position of the guide along x is 300 units. At frame 17, the guide is at 100 units; the character's foot moves a total of 200 units per step (300 – 100 = 200). This value is known as the stride length. Doubling it equals 400 units for the total cycle. On the first frame, move the floor to the starting position. On the last frame (frame 33), move the floor 400 units along the x axis. In-between these frames linearly. That's it. The shot is done.

On the CD

On the CD is a finished movie of the walk. The title is TINK-WALK.AVI or TINKWALK.MOV for Mac; you can watch it as a reference, if you like.

Exercise #3: Animating a Walk Using Inverse Kinematics

Inverse kinematics is by far the most popular way to animate the lower body. IK is one of the preferred walk-animation methods because it ensures that a character's grounded foot stays in the same spot for the duration of the step. Knowing that the feet are locked frees the animator's mind from annoying details and enables him to concentrate on more important things, such as posing the character.

Implementation of IK differs between packages, but most software enables you to constrain an IK chain to an effector that resides outside the hierarchy of the skeleton. This exercise has the leg chains constrained at the ankle to outside effectors. These effectors, in turn, parent the feet chains. Animating an object outside the hierarchy of the skeleton has an advantage because moving the hips does not affect the position of the feet.

As with the previous walk, this walk is timed at 16 frames per step, 32 for one full cycle.

1. Start with a neutral skeleton.

  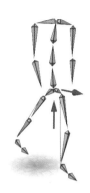  

2. Start with the lower body. Create the first pose on the first frame. Position the left ankle forward, the right ankle back. Position the hips halfway between the feet. Rotate the hips along the vertical axis so that the left hip is slightly forward. Set position and rotation keys for all these objects.

3. Move the slider to frame 8 to get the passing pose. Move the hips forward so that they are directly over the left ankle. Move the hips up so that the left leg extends to nearly straight. Rotate the hips along the vertical axis back to zero. Set position and rotation keys for the hip.

4. Position the right leg. Move the right ankle so that it is directly above the left ankle and slightly below the left knee. Set a position key for the right ankle.

 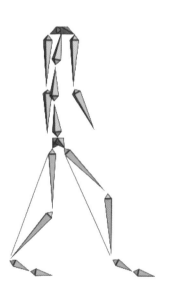

5. Create a pose that is the mirror of the first. Place the right ankle forward so that the foot rests firmly on the ground. Move the hips forward and down so that they are halfway between the feet. Rotate the hips along the vertical axis so that the right hip is slightly forward. Set position and rotation keys for all these objects. Also set a position key for the left foot. Scrubbing the animation

continues

Exercise: continued

6. Now tweak the step. Go back to frame 4, the recoil position, where the hips sink as the weight is transferred to the forward foot. Move the hips down at this point and set a position key.

7. At the recoil position, the left foot needs to be rotated slightly downward. Rotate the foot and set a rotation key.

8. From a front view, go to frame 8, the middle of the cycle. The hips should now be rotated slightly to the right due to the weight of the free right leg. Rotate the hips and set a rotation key. Move the hips slightly to the left to place the weight of the body toward the left leg. Scrubbing the animation should now show a basic lower body step.

9. Move on to the upper body, starting with the spine. At frame 1, rotate the joints of the spine so that the shoulders mirror the hips. Set rotation keys for the spine.

10. Move to frame 8, the middle of the first step. Rotate the spine so the shoulders are even with the hips when viewed from above. From the front, rotate the spine so that the shoulders mirror the hips. Set rotation keys for the spine.

11. Move to frame 16. Adjust the spine so that it mirrors the pose on frame 1. Set rotation keys for the spine. The step is almost complete.

12. Move on to the arms. With the right leg forward, the right arm needs to be back. Conversely, the left arm needs to be forward. Set rotation keys for these objects. Move to frame 16 and mirror these poses, setting rotation keys once again.

Repeat steps 1–12 to create the left step. When finished, render a test.

Rather than working a step at a time, in actual production, you probably want to block out all the steps first. Next, you move on to the upper body and set all the keys for a full cycle, and then copy these keys for the duration of the walk.

On the CD

On the CD is a test of this walk. It is titled IKWALK.AVI or IKWALK.MOV for Mac.

Exercise #4: Animating a Walk Using Inverse or Broken Hierarchies

In this example, you animate a walk using inverse hierarchies. This method works well in almost any package. One nice thing about it is that this method locks down the feet quite easily and forces you to move the hips properly. Also, you can animate this walk straight-ahead rather than in a cycle. Animate this walk at 12 frames per step for film (15 frames per step for video).

You will show this walk on a standard skeleton for reference. The one thing you will notice is that it is difficult to align the hips exactly with the tops of the legs. Because of this, this type of walk is best for nonsegmented characters. An ideal character is one where the hips are concealed, such as a woman in a skirt. This method can also work with a deformation program, because

slight gaps between the legs and hips will usually not show up on the deformed mesh.

Begin by getting the hierarchies set up properly. The hierarchy for the leg is broken at the hips. For each leg, the toe parents the foot, which parents the shin and then the thigh. It is the exact opposite of the standard skeleton, but can still be animated quite easily.

1. Set up the bones (or segments) on the right leg so that the toes are at the top of the hierarchy. The order of the hierarchy is as follows: toes parent the heel, then the shin, and then the thigh. Do the same for the left leg.

You now have three separate hierarchies: two legs and a standard skeleton with no legs.

2. Your main task is to animate the legs and feet. Leave the body out of the shot for this part, because it won't be needed until later. Position the legs in the extended position, with the right leg forward. To adjust the positions of the legs, move the toes first, and then work your way up the chain from there. The position of the legs determines the stride length. Also, be sure that the tops of the legs are not too far apart, where the "hips" would be.

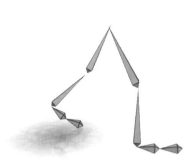 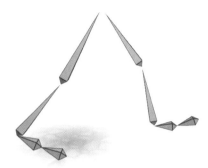 

3. Now you can animate the rest of the walk. On the right leg, rotate the toe and move the foot so it contacts the ground. From this point, the foot remains stable until the next step is taken. Notice how you can rotate the joints of the leg without affecting the position of the foot. The feet stay put and no slipping occurs.

4. Jump forward to frame 13—the beginning of the next step. Move the left foot into the extended position and rotate (don't move) the toe of the right foot to the proper position.

   Go back through the first step and align the rest of the keys.

5. Align the passing position. Go to frame 7, which is halfway through the first step, and rotate the right shin at the ankle to make the leg almost vertical. Rotate the left leg so the foot is some-what vertical and position the thigh by rotating the knee. The tops of the right and left legs should be about equal, with the left slightly lower.

6. Go to frame 4 and get the recoil position. Again, rotate the right leg at the ankle so that the knee is bent. Rotate and align the left foot so that the leg is free.

7. Create a key near frame 10, where the left foot swings forward. Because the hierar-chy is backward, positioning the free leg may be a little tricky.

8. Play through the first step and tweak the keys.

9. You now have the first step. By repeating this procedure, you can continue and create as many more steps as you want. Animate three or four more steps. When you're fin-ished, you should have a nice pair of legs walking across the floor.

continues

Exercise: continued

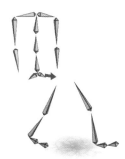

10. Now that you have the legs and feet, all you have to do is place the body above them and rock it back and forth so that the hips of the body skeleton match up with the tops of the legs.

   On the first frame, position the body so it is above the legs, with the hips aligned with the legs. Rotate the spine to give it a natural stance.

13. Continue through the rest of the shot, positioning the hips above the legs and rotating them from right to left along with the tops of the legs.

14. Play back the animation to make sure that the character remains centered above the legs.

11. Move to the next set of keys, at the recoil position (frame 3). Position the hips above the legs, but lower. If you animated the feet and legs properly, you should naturally see how to position the hips.

15. Animate the arms. As in the previous example, you need to have them drag slightly behind the action of the legs. When the right leg is forward, the right arm is back, and vice versa.

16. Finally, render the animation and tweak as necessary.

12. Next is the passing position. In this position, the left side is slightly lower at the hip, so rotate the hips slightly in this direction.

Beyond Walking

All these exercises have shown how to create a basic walk. There are plenty of other ways to get around besides a walk. Characters may also run, skip, sneak, shuffle, and tiptoe, among many walking variations. Within these gaits, each character's personality will also come through in the walk. Many animators think the walk is one of the key parts of a character's personality. John Wayne's walk is completely different than Groucho Marx's, for example. Knowing the character means knowing the walk. With that in mind, let's analyze a few other types of locomotion.

The Run

A run is more than just a fast and highly exaggerated walk. Instead of continuous falling, it's best to view a run as continuous leaping, with the body tending to lean forward a lot more. In a walk, one foot is always on the ground; in a run, there are times when both feet are airborne. The stride length also increases, making this distance longer than the feet could normally reach in a walk.

The timing of a run is faster than a walk, and can get down to a few frames per step. If you're animating an extremely fast run, motion blur is absolutely required to keep the feet and legs from strobing. Take a look at a running character and see the differences between a walk and a run.

On the CD

On the CD are four animations that will show you this run from four different views. These files are called RUN1.AVI through RUN4.AVI (Mac users should load RUN1.MOV through RUN4.MOV.) Watch these animations for reference.

This figure illustrates the "contact position." Notice that the body leans forward, and the legs are farther apart than they are during a walk.

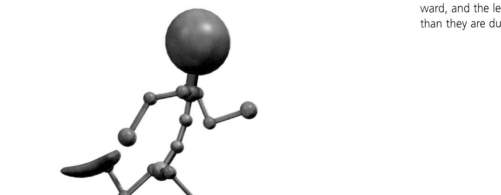

After contact is made, the forward leg absorbs the shock of the body at the recoil position. As in walking, this point is the lowest position in the cycle. Because the body is moving faster, momentum is increased, causing the bent leg to be even more exaggerated. The body is over the planted foot to help balance the weight.

This figure illustrates a position similar to the passing position, because it is halfway through the step. At this point in the cycle, the grounded foot pushes the body upward.

The body is now airborne and is at the highest point in the cycle.

The body lands and the next step starts. As in the walk, the second half of the cycle should be a mirror of the first. The body is over the planted foot to help distribute the weight.

The Skip

Another gait that is completely different from walking is the skip. In a skip, the character takes off and lands on the same leg, and then switches legs for the next step. Even though the foot pattern is changed, the concepts of weight and balance do not. The character's hips, shoulders, and spine all move in concert to keep the skeleton in balance.

This skip, animated by Angie Jones, shows the basic foot and body movements. The skip starts much like the walk, with the feet apart. A skip happens primarily on the toes, however.

As in the walk, the weight is transferred to the forward foot (or in this case, the forward toe).

The foot pushes off, sending the character into a small leap or hop. The opposite foot moves forward as the hips rotate.

In the middle of the leap, the back leg moves forward slightly. The forward leg remains high and tucks under the body.

The character lands, but on the rear foot, with the forward foot staying high.

The forward foot touches down, and the cycle repeats as a mirror of the first step.

The Sneak

Another favorite walk is the standard sneak. If you analyze it, this is just a variation of the basic walk, but the character is walking on his toes. It is a good example of how the basic walk can be modified to show character and mood. The main goal of a sneak is to walk quietly.

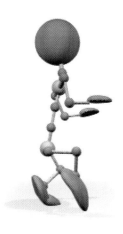

This sneak, animated by Angie Jones, starts much like the standard walk, but with the character on his toes. This makes the character slightly off center, so he extends his arms to regain balance.

The recoil position. Notice how the feet stay very close to the ground to help maintain balance.

The passing position. In the sneak, the planted leg does not extend nearly as much as in the walk.

Before the passing leg touches down, the character leans over at the waist to help maintain balance.

The cycle is finished and ready for the next leg.

Animating Four-Legged Walks

If you think mastering a two-legged walk is difficult, you'll find a four-legged walk doubly troublesome. First, the anatomy of most four-legged animals (as well as birds and dinosaurs) is quite different from primate anatomy.

Take a horse, for example. The horse actually walks on its toes. Whereas the human heel actually touches the ground, the horse's "heel" is far above the ground—where the human knee would be. The horse's knee is actually even higher up, as are the thigh and hip. The front legs are similar to human arms. Again, the horse walks on his fingers and his wrist is far above the ground.

To create a realistic four-legged walk, you need to study the movements of real animals. Take a video camera to the zoo, or rent a nature documentary and go through the animal's movements, frame by frame.

In addition to normal walking, a four-legged animal has several different gaits. The animal varies the timing and rhythm of its steps as it moves faster and faster. These gaits are the walk, trot, canter, and gallop. Some animals, however, may do only a subset of these. The elephant, for example, always walks—it never changes its gait. It simply walks slower or faster.

In the walk, the horse's legs behave very much like the arms and legs of a human—if the right rear leg is back, the right front leg is forward, with the opposite happening on the left. This positioning changes as the strides change. By the time the horse has reached a full gallop, the front legs are in sync, going forward and back nearly in unison. The back legs operate the same way.

The walk.

The gallop.

Another way to view a four-legged walk is in a more cartoonish way. Think of the old vaudeville act where two guys get into a tattered old horse suit. On stage, the horse literally walks like two people stitched together. You animate the walk like a double–two-legged walk, forcing you to have different joint constraints and body construction.

The back legs on this dog are not realistic; they bend the same way human legs do. Still, the cartoon nature of its design enables the animator to move the dog this way and get away with it.

A cartoonish four-legged character is much simpler to animate, because you can set up its walk like a double–two-legged walk.

Conclusion

Walking is a very technical animation task, involving weight, balance, and motion. As you master the syntax of walks and runs, move on to adding the subtleties of character. Each of your characters will walk a bit differently, depending on its personality. Like a musician who learns his scales and then learns to improvise, a walk is a fundamental building block for animators to improvise upon.

CHAPTER 10

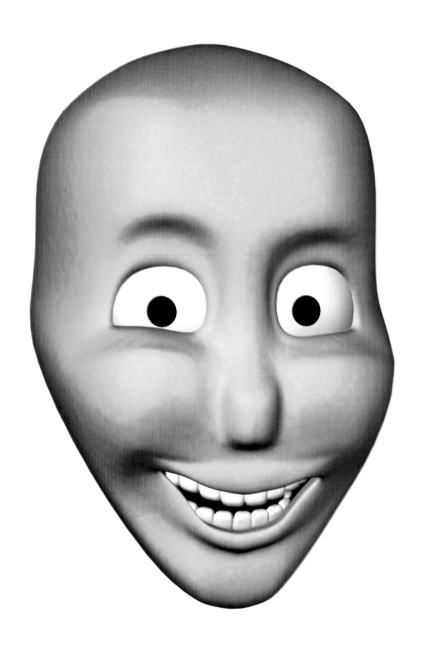

Facial Animation and Dialogue

Animating the face is one of the most challenging and rewarding tasks you will encounter as an animator. We humans are all experts in the subtleties of expression and emotion. We know instinctively when a bad actor is on the screen—typically, because his emotions seem forced rather than genuine. The same goes for animation; great facial animation looks seamless and does not draw attention to itself, whereas bad animation seems curiously "off" for some unknown reason.

Animating the face requires a good eye and a thorough knowledge of acting and emotion. While you are in the learning process, keep a keen eye on people, their faces, and how they express themselves. A good background in classic films—particularly those of the silent comedians, who had to express themselves purely through facial expressions and body language—can prove invaluable to the animator.

Additionally, good software tools are a must. You need a package that can build and animate complex shapes with a minimum of fuss. A well-modeled head that is flexible and animates simply will save you a couple of bottles of aspirin down the road.

Methods for Animating the Face

Over the years, many methods have been used to animate the face. Early in computer graphics, some people tugged and pulled the vertices of the face, frame by agonizing frame, to get animation. Later, other people deformed the face directly through the used of bones, clusters, and lattices. All these methods have their place, but they all have a number of weaknesses, most important of which is the lack of control over the subtle details of the shape of the face.

Over time, most people learned that the best way to control these subtle details is in a modeling program, not a deformation module. The only method that takes advantage of the modeling program is called *morphing*. In most productions, morphing has become the de facto standard method for animating faces.

Morphing

Morphing can create very complex facial animation. Although other methods are still used, morphing is very powerful and fairly easy to control. Much of the facial animation exercises in this book concentrate on the use of morphing.

Morphing changes the shape of the base object into the shape of other, target, objects. Setting up your character for animation is simply a matter of using your program's modeler to work up a library of the appropriate facial poses. This has distinct advantages, because each shape can be refined to perfection in the modeling program, rather than at animation time.

Morphing works for both patch and polygonal models. Some packages force you to create separate objects for the shapes, whereas some enable you to create shapes by using one model. Most software packages require that the models being morphed contain the same number of vertices in the same order, a task easily accomplished by modeling a single, stock, expressionless face, copying it, and reworking it into the many expressions and facial poses you need. There are two basic methods for creating morphs: single and multiple target morphing.

Single-Target Morphing

A *single-target morphing* system allows only transition between two discrete shapes. This forces the animator to model all the possible poses ahead of time, which discourages experimentation. You also can't do simple overlapping actions, such as closing the mouth while opening the eyes. This results in animation that seems stiff at best. Most decent software these days offer the more-sophisticated feature of multiple-target morphing.

Multiple-Target Morphing

Multiple-target morphing (also known as *shape weights* and *blend shape*) enables mixing multiple shapes. It enables you to model individual shapes for parts of the face that smile, open the jaw, raise the eyebrows, and so on. You can then combine these shapes for a pose that is a smiling face, with the jaw 50% open and the eyebrows raised 30%. This makes manipulating the face quite easy. Each morph target moves only part of the face, with the facial expression derived by mixing all the parts. You can combine as many shapes as you want. All you really need to animate are the relative weights of the shapes, making it much easier to create the perfect pose for a given moment and also requiring that fewer poses be modeled. Most packages these days even allow you to attach these weights to virtual sliders so that you can "dial in" your poses, which makes generating poses at animation time downright easy.

Modeling Morph Targets for Animation

The best way to model morph targets for animation is to study the underlying anatomy of the face. Recall from Chapter 5, "Modeling Heads for Animation," how the muscles move the face. In a multiple-target morph, because poses can be mixed, all that needs to be modeled are the extremes of the individual muscles. Because each muscle is connected to the face in a specific place, flexing just that muscle changes the shape of only part of the face. If you model that exact shape, you have an anatomically correct animation when all the shapes (all the muscles) are mixed together.

Ideally, you could model targets for every muscle in the face, which amounts to several dozen targets. For ease of use, this book outlines a dozen or so of the most useful shapes. Although some of these poses combine several muscles, the theory is the same: Each slider controls only part of the face. When modeling for a morph system, be careful to move only those vertices that need to be affected by any particular muscle. If you accidentally move a vertex on the ear, for example, a character's ear may change shape every time the jaw opens. Also be sure to make smooth transitions from the right to left sides of the face. If you model a right smile, make sure that the smile transitions smoothly to the left side of the face, and vice versa. If the same part of the face is manipulated by more than one slider, you may get unwanted results, such as a top lip that goes bonkers when both smile sliders are moved.

Also remember that these poses are extremes, so be sure to model them as such. Try to imagine the biggest smile, the saddest frown, and so on. Try looking in the mirror and use your own face as reference.

Lower-Face Poses

Lower-face poses are centered around the mouth, although some, such as the smile and sneer, affect the eyes a bit. Lower-face poses are usually used for lip sync, but can also be a part of many other expressions.

The first pose is the neutral face. Model it with the eyes open and the jaw slightly slack, leaving the mouth open. All the other poses will be derived from this basic face.

The next pose is the open jaw. This is modeled by selecting the vertices of the lower face, and then moving them down and slightly back to simulate the effect of the jaw rotating open.

The pursed lip, or oooh shape, is the product of the obicularis oris muscle. When modeling this shape, be sure to maintain volume in the lips, which get slightly thicker as the muscle contracts.

Smiles are primarily the action of the zygomatic major muscle. In a smile, the corner of the mouth is pulled up into the cheek, which tends to puff out. In an extreme smile, the cheek creates an arc, which cuts into the bottom edge of the eye.

This frown is a combination of the triangularis and depressor labii inferioris muscles. Basically, these muscles work to pull the corner of the mouth down.

The sneer is the product of the levator labii superioris muscle. It pulls the lip up toward the edge of the nose. It also affects the skin along the side of the nose all the way up to the corner of the eye.

Upper-Face Poses

It has often been said that the eyes are the mirror to the soul. Although many animators may concentrate on the mouth and lip sync, true emotion is communicated through the eyes, brows, and upper face. Getting good upper-face animation is critically important to any facial animation.

The corrugator pulls the brow down and in toward the bridge of the nose. In an extreme position, the character looks angry, although this shape is used for many other emotions.

Left and right eyebrows are manipulated by the frontalis. Each brow is modeled separately to get maximum control.

If your character has eyelids as part of the face, a left and right blink also need to be modeled.

On the CD

All these face shapes are located on the CD.

Upper-Face Poses for Stylized Characters

Some characters are modeled without fleshy eyebrows and lids. These characters can be still be manipulated to get upper-face poses. Typically, a character may be modeled with simple spheres for eyes and a hemisphere for a lid. By rotating the lids to different angles, you can still get the effect of a brow.

Other Facial Poses

In addition to the poses mentioned in the last sections, any number of custom poses can be modeled to get just the expression you need. If the sliders don't give you the face you need, the best advice is to get the face as close as you can, fix it, copy the new head to make another target, and use the new target as the face for that particular moment.

Not all characters have fleshy eyes. These eyes are made from simple spheres with the lids as hemispheres.

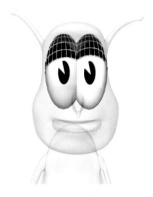

They are simply placed inside this character's head…

…to make cartoonish eyes.

If the lids are rotated outward, you get one expression.

Rotate them inward, you get another expression. In this case, the lids take the place of the brows.

This pose simply closes the lips. It can be helpful in dialogue or when tweaking a pose.

This pose tucks the bottom lip under the front teeth to get the sound of the letter F. It is used in dialogue.

In addition to custom poses, there are a few more stock poses you can model to complete your inventory. These are not mandatory, but they do come in handy.

Assigning Targets

After the targets are modeled, getting them to animate is simply a matter of assigning them as morph targets. How this is done depends on your software, so consult your manual on the exact keystrokes. When assigning, it is a good idea to keep the targets grouped logically within the interface. With 10–20 sliders to contend with, it's much more efficient if the right smile slider is located next to the left smile slider, for example. Keep lower- and upper-face targets together for the same reason.

Manipulating the Face

After the targets are assigned, the fun can begin. Most software provides sliders, which make manipulating a face quite easy. If the targets were modeled correctly, manipulating the face is as simple as moving sliders. As fun as it can be, you still need to understand some basics of how facial expressions are manipulated and how facial expressions convey emotion.

Pushing Poses

Most software packages enable you to manipulate a slider beyond the range of 0–100%. This means that your big smile can be even bigger if you move it above 100% to, for example, 125%. When a vertex is morphed, the software simply moves it along a path to its new location; so when a brow raises, for example, the vertices representing the brow move along a line to their new position. If the slider is at 50%, the vertex travels halfway to the new position. At 125%, it is beyond the position, but along the same line.

This technique can be very handy, but you will find that there is a point past 100% where the surface of the face will begin to break up, or the pose will simply look unnatural. If your poses are already pushed, this may happen just above 100%. Still, this little technique is great for getting a little bit more out of your character.

Negative Sliders

Another trick is to push the sliders below zero into negative territory. This simply causes the vertices to move in the opposite direction, but along the same line as before. This can enable some of your poses to do double duty. For example, if you push the jaw slider below zero, the mouth closes, which may eliminate the need for a closed mouth pose.

Another good example is the center brow. When positive, the slider indicates anger. When it is pushed into negative territory, it raises the brow, which creates a worried expression. The right and left brow can also be used in such a manner. Pushing the blink sliders into negative territory opens the eyes wide.

Some poses, however, do not behave well when pushed into negative territory. A negative smile will not make a frown, for example. Sneers and frowns are also too specific to work well when pushed into negative territory.

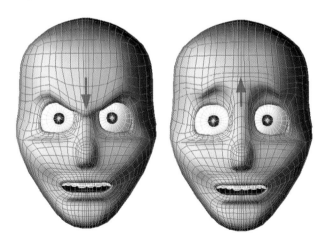

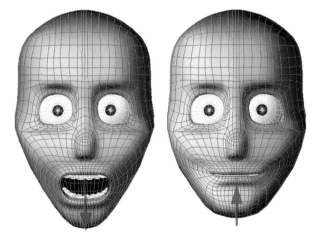

The center brow also works along the same lines. Positive values show anger, and negative values show worry.

When the jaw slider is moved into positive territory, the jaw opens. Negative values make the jaw close.

Creating Facial Expressions

The reason you manipulate the sliders is to create facial expressions. Expressions are much like the body poses that an animator uses to help a character act and carry off a scene. When building an expression, always ask yourself what the character is feeling at the moment. This helps guide you to create the correct face.

Basic Expressions

The face can make an infinite number of expressions; luckily, they fall into some broad categories: anger, disgust, fear, joy, sadness, and surprise. I'll detail them here, but you must recognize that they are extreme expressions only—primary colors among the many hues of expression. You could never animate with these six alone, but understanding these basic "faces" can take you a long way toward understanding the under-lying mechanics of expression.

Anger: The eyes are open, but the brows are down. The mouth is usually open with the lips tensed and teeth bared. The jaw may be lowered.

Disgust: The whole face is tightened, with the eyes nar-rowed and center brow lowered slightly. The mouth is closed and the upper lip pulled into a sneer.

Fear: The mouth is wide open and pulled back at the lower corners. The jaw is dropped, and the eyes are wide, with the brows raised.

Joy: The mouth is pulled upward into a smile, exposing the upper teeth, forcing the cheeks up. The brows are usually relaxed.

Sadness: The mouth is pulled down at the lower corners and may expose the lower teeth. The eyes squint, and when crying, may be closed. The brow is raised only in the middle.

Surprise: The eyes are wide open, and the brows are raised but not furrowed. The mouth is relaxed, and the jaw is slack.

The Brows and Expression

Remember that the upper part of the face is the most important part of an expression. One way to change the meaning of an expression quickly is to manipulate the brow. The position of the brow probably conveys more information about emotion than any other part of the face. When brows are lowered, it usually indicates dark emotions—anger, for example. When raised, the face becomes more open.

Changing the brow changes emotion. With brows raised, the character looks happy.

With the same mouth, but brows lowered, he looks evil.

Symmetry and Expression

The expressions we've looked at so far have been fairly symmetrical. When animating the face, it's always best to introduce asymmetry into the poses to make things look more natural. Just as when posing the body, the dreaded twins can creep into facial animation as well, making your face look stale and boring. Still, you need to be careful not to make things too asymmetrical or it will change the meaning of the expression.

When the face pose becomes extremely asymmetrical, the expressions become less clear. If a character flashes a crooked smile, for example, it usually means he's not sincere. If one eyebrow is raised, it can indicate curiosity or insight. Of course, if your character needs to express such emotions, this knowledge can work to your advantage.

This symmetrical face is nice, but not very interesting.

Lowering the left smile a bit introduces asymmetry and makes the face more natural.

Lower it too much, however, and the meaning of the expression changes.

Complex Expressions

Many expressions are not as distinct as the ones indicated previously. Of course, the palette of human emotions is broad with many subtle hues. Many times, facial expressions are asymmetrical, and many times they combine various attributes of the basic expressions. A smiling mouth with lowered brows might indicate evil, for example.

When creating these expressions, remember the basics learned from the fundamental expressions. Because the eyes are the most important to conveying emotion, start with the eyes. Much as with the hips in the body, if you get the eyes right, the rest of the pose falls into place. If you ever get confused as to what the expression should be, look in the mirror and try to mimic the expression.

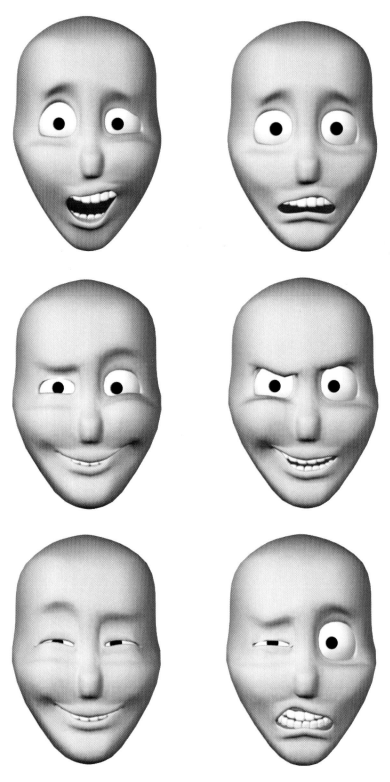

Many complex expressions can be made simply by manipulating the sliders.

Animating the Head and Face

When the face is set up and you understand how to pose a face to get expressions, you are ready to animate. Those who are learning facial animation should not start with learning to animate dialogue, but with the simple act of conveying emotion. You do not need to have a character speak for it to be expressive. There are plenty of examples of characters who express themselves quite well without dialogue.

Animating the Head

Before you animate the face itself, you need to study the head and how it moves. A perfectly animated face on a perfectly still head looks horrible. Head motions are necessary to accent and emphasize the facial animation. If a character is talking, his head nods or bobs to accent certain lines of dialogue. If a character is curious, he may cock his head to one side. If the character is disapproving, the head may shake as if to say "no." If a character turns his head, it usually suggests a shift of attention or focus. (As was mentioned in Chapter 8, "Basics of Character Animation," the head always turns along an arc. When the head turns from left to right, it usually dips in the middle of the turn.)

Also remember the principles of animation. If a character turns his head to the right, he anticipates it with a slight turn to the left. The character may overshoot the turn slightly and settle in. All the principles of animation apply equally to the head and face as they do to the body.

Eye Direction

Because the eyes are the most important part of the face, where the eyes are pointed is a very important bit of information. Be sure to have your character's eyes firmly fixed on the subject at hand. If your character is talking to someone, but the eyes are looking off into the distance, your character will appear as if it's staring into space and not paying attention. Of course, this can be used as an effect, but typically you want your characters to be looking at the people they're talking to.

Another little tidbit of human interaction is that even when a person moves his or her head slightly—to accentuate a part of speech, for example—the eyes tend to remain fixed on their target.

"Look At" Functions

Most packages have functions that enable you to constrain an object's direction so that it's pointed at another. Some packages call this function a "look at" controller, because it forces the object to always face or look at the object to which it is constrained. When such a controller is applied to the pupils of the eye, for example, the eyes automatically rotate to track an object.

One good example is a fly buzzing around the room. By constraining the pupils of the eyes so they always look at the fly, you can make the fly go all over the place and the character's eyes always follow it. This example is extreme, but the principle applies even to a situation as simple as two people talking face to face, each character's eyes fixed on the other. You simply have each character's eyes look at the other character's face.

A much more flexible way to use the same function is to create an invisible null or dummy object to help define your character's focus. Simply make your character's eyes look at this invisible object. You can then move the object anywhere in the scene and rest assured your character's eyes will be pointed exactly where you want them.

In this scene, the character's pupils are fixed to the red sphere with a "look at" controller.

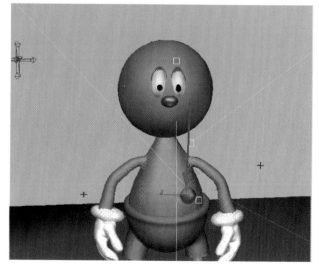

When the sphere moves down, the pupils follow, remaining fixed on the sphere. Making the sphere invisible enables you to use it to guide the eyes in any shot. Simply place it where you want your character to look, and the eyes will follow.

Pointy Objects

Another way to keep the eye on target is to stick pointy objects in your character's eyes. No, I don't want you to maim your characters. By pointy objects, I simply mean an invisible object used as a guide to assist in pointing the eyes. Usually, you use a thin cone or a cylinder that has a transparent texture applied to it so that it doesn't show up when rendering.

To create such a guide, simply model a long, thin cone or a cylinder and attach it to the pupil via a hierarchy or a constraint. The guides will then point out into space like searchlights, showing the direction of the character's gaze. If the pupil turns, so will the guide, giving you a very good idea as to where the eyes are pointed and helping you aim them at their target.

Blinks

Blinks go a long way to adding life to your character. Generally, you should have your character blink every few seconds just to show it's alive. The timing of the blink itself depends on your character's personality and mood. A really fast blink might take 4 frames, and a normal blink will take 6–8. A 20-frame blink may mean that the character is very sleepy or very dumb.

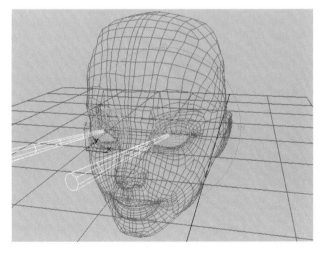

In this wireframe view, you see how these simple cones help position the eyes.

If you turn off the cones to rendering (or apply an invisible texture to them), they disappear after rendering.

This figure illustrates the standard timing for a blink. This should work well for most situations.

This blink's timing is fast, but it will make a character more alert.

This blink takes much longer and is for a very large or very sleepy character.

Blinks and Squash

Another trick, particularly with cartoonish characters, is to squash the eyes as they blink. This will help exaggerate the motion and bring the blink to life. The squash can be done in any number of the methods mentioned in Chapters 5 and 8. Many people simply scale the eyes, but some use lattices around the eye hierarchy to get better control of the shape.

To get a little bit more bounce to the blink, another trick is to over-shoot the shape at the end of the blink. Let's say you have a blink of 8 frames. At the bottom of the blink on frame 4, the eyes should be squashed. At the end of the blink on frame 8, make the eyes slightly taller, and then settle in to the final pose on frame 10. This also works for more realistic eyes; simply move the shape sliders into negative values so that the eye gets slightly wider for 2 frames at the end of the blink.

Blinks and Head Turns

During a head turn, most people tend to blink. Adding a blink in your character's head turns will make him seem more alive. Another little tid-bit is that characters tend to look in the direction of the head turn, so it's best to lead the turn with the eyes. If the head is turning left, the eyes will turn left before the head turns.

To get added life from a blink, squash the shape of the eyes at the bottom of the blink and then overshoot the final shape by a few frames.

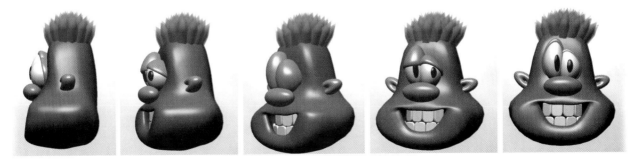

The eyes usually point in the direction of the head turn, and a blink in the middle adds some life.

Blinks and Eye Direction

One problem that often crops up is a character with a lazy eye. This is an eye that seems to float rather than appear to be locked on a specific target. Some of these problems are poor eye direction, and others can be fixed with a simple blink. When people change the direction of their gaze, it is almost always accompanied by a blink. If your character looks from left to right, add a blink as the eyes change direction. The blink will help the eyes look less "floaty."

There are times when a character's eyes need to travel without blinking. One good example is when a character is reading. In that case, the eyes go from left to right without a blink. Remember, like the head, the eyes move along arcs, dipping slightly in the middle of a turn.

Overlap in Facial Animation

One of the big reasons that multiple target morphing is used in facial animation is because it gives you the ability to overlap the actions of the face. Just as with the body, actions do not happen all at once in facial animation. A character may need to smile as he's talking, for instance, or perhaps change the position of the brows.

One tip is to let one side of the face lead the other. If a character smiles, the left side of the face may begin the smile a frame or two ahead of the right. Also, as is the case with head turns, the eyes tend to take the lead in facial animation. If a change of mood happens, the change usually begins with a change in the expression of the eyes.

Exercise #1: Facial Animation Test

To understand how facial animation works, do a simple test where a character changes his emotion through the simple use of expression. Make a character go from happy to sad, curious to shocked, or worried to fearful, for example. Be sure to use blinks, as well as head and body motion, to accentuate the shift.

Animating Lip-Sync

Animating lip sync can really frighten the beginning animator—and rightly so—because it's one of the most difficult techniques for an animator to master. Live-action people have it easy; they just point the cameras at the actors and ask them to speak. Re-creating natural lip movements in animation, however, requires a great deal of time, patience, and analysis. In addition to getting the mouth shapes and positions right, you must be concerned with the acting and body motions associated with the dialogue. As with any hard task, however, animating lip sync is grounded in some simple techniques. Practice those techniques and you'll be on your way to mastering lip sync.

As you have seen, facial animation is a lot more than just moving the mouth. When animating a shot, it is very important to create facial animation in layers. Do not do it all at once; begin with the dialogue. When a character speaks dialogue, the shape and position of the mouth is perhaps 10–20% of the total effect. After the character is speaking with a neutral face, layer in the eyes and brows and then the rest of the facial animation, moving onto each as you finish the first. This keeps the facial animation from being mushy. Equally as important to the audience is the movement of the body and head. For the purposes of this book, let's start the process with the mouth.

Recording Dialogue

In animation, dialogue is almost always recorded before the characters are drawn. Dialogue looks more natural when the animator follows the natural rhythms of speech. Voice actors have difficulty matching previously animated dialogue while trying to make the dialogue sound natural, which is why recording the speech before animation begins is essential.

Directing a voice session is an art in itself, but the voice actors must know the scene and the setting. This knowledge enables the actors to inflect different tones and pauses into their speech. It also is useful for timing purposes if the actors act out character movements as they record the dialogue. If the voice actor does this, it might be a good idea to videotape the voice session. You can then play the tape to provide additional reference for your animation of both dialogue and gestures. Another method that may prove useful is to give the actors a storyboard so they can visualize the shot as they record the dialogue.

After the dialogue is recorded, the animator is responsible for breaking down the track, frame by frame, into individual phonemes (the most basic sounds of human speech) to be animated. The easiest way to picture a phoneme is to think of each discrete sound that makes up a word. The word "funny," for example, has four phonemes: the f sound, the uh sound, an n sound, and a long e. Reading a dialogue track can be a tedious task. The dialogue must be broken down frame by frame and written by hand onto exposure sheets. Computer animators have the advantage of using digital audio software to read their tracks, and some packages are now attaining the capability of performing voice recognition and can actually break down the track automatically.

The exposure sheet is used to break down the dialogue track, frame by frame. Here a character is saying, "Give it a shot" (highlighted in white). The exposure sheet can also contain other information. To the left of the dialogue is a column in which to write notes on how you want your characters to act—to blink or bob the head, for example. To the right of the dialogue are notes indicating which mouth shapes to use.

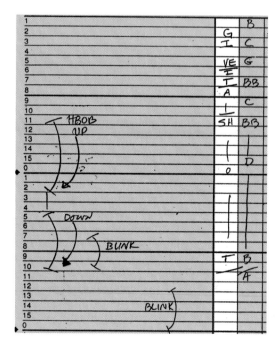

The Eight Basic Mouth Positions

Before reading the track, however, you must first understand how the mouth moves when it speaks. There are dozens of different mouth shapes made during the course of normal speech. Animators usually boil these down to a handful of standard shapes that are used repeatedly. Depending on the style of animation, some animators get away with as few as three or four shapes, and some may use dozens. For most situations, you can get away with approximately eight basic mouth positions. These eight positions usually provide adequate coverage and give you the ability to animate most dialogue effectively.

To really see how these positions work, watch yourself in the mirror while you talk. Make the sounds used by each position. If you talk naturally, you'll begin to see how the shapes work and how they all fit together into a continuous stream. The shapes and the rules that govern them are certainly not strict. Different accents and speech patterns may cause you to substitute one shape for the other in order to achieve a more convincing look.

You may notice that some of these positions are not in the standard library of shapes you modeled as morph targets. They can, however, be created at animation time by mixing the appropriate sliders. One good example is the sound of the word "Oh," which is created by mixing together an open jaw with the oooh sound. In fact, for speech, most of the grunt work is done by manipulating only these two shapes, with a possible ffff thrown in when needed. Other sliders—such as smile, frown, and sneer—are used mainly to add character to the face.

Position A is the closed mouth used for consonants made by the lips, specifically the M, B, and P sounds. Typically, this can be made by pushing the open jaw pose into negative territory to close the mouth. In this position, the lips are usually their normal width. For added realism, you could mix in an additional shape to get the lips slightly pursed for sounds following an oooh sound, such as in the word "room."

Position B has the mouth open with the teeth closed. This position is a common shape and is used for consonants made within the mouth, specifically sounds made by C, D, G, K, N, R, S, TH, Y, and Z. All these sounds can also be made with the teeth slightly open, particularly in fast speech.

Position C is used for the wide open vowels, such as A and I. It is essentially the same as the fundamental shape for an open jaw.

Position D is used primarily for the vowel E, but it can also be used on occasion for C, K, or N during fast speech.

Position E has the mouth wide open in an elliptical shape. This is the position used for the vowel O, as in the word "flow." It is created by mixing together an open jaw and the oooh sound. Sometimes, particularly when the sound is at the end of a word, you can overlap this shape with the one in Position F to close the mouth.

Position F has the mouth smaller, but more pursed. Position F is used for the oooh sound, as in food, and for the vowel U. It is one of the fundamental mouth shapes.

Position G has the mouth wide open with the tongue against the teeth. This position is reserved for the letter L, but can also be used for D or TH sounds, particularly when preceded by A or I. It is essentially an open jaw with the tongue moved up against the top teeth. If speech is particularly rapid, this shape may not be necessary; substitute Position B.

Position H has the bottom lip tucked under the teeth to make the sound of the letters F or V. In highly pronounced speech, this shape is necessary, but the shape could also be replaced with Position B for more casual or rapid speech. This shape is one of the extra shapes modeled previously.

Reading the Track

Now that you understand the basic mouth positions, it's time to break down the track. If you have animator's exposure sheet paper, use it. Otherwise, get a pad of lined paper on which to write your track, using one line per frame. (If you prefer, you can create a spreadsheet for this purpose and do it all digitally.) Load the dialogue into a sound editing program. A number of sound editing packages are available, and you should choose one that enables you to display the time in frames, as well as select and play portions of the track. The ability to label sections in the editor is also handy.

The first thing you should do is match your sound editing program's time base to the time base you're animating—30, 25, or 24fps, for example. After your time base is set, selecting a snippet consisting of a few frames of dialogue should enable you to listen to the dialogue a word or phoneme at a time and read each phoneme's exact length on the editor's data window.

The visual readout of the dialogue gives you clues as to where the words start and stop. Work your way through the track and write down each phoneme as it occurs on your exposure sheet, frame by frame. This is a tedious but necessary chore.

Some packages give you the ability to play back audio in sync with the animation. This feature is particularly helpful because you may be able to skip the step of reading the track and simply eyeball the sync. Still, it's always a good idea to read the track methodically before animating so that you completely understand the track and know exactly where all the sounds occur.

When reading the track, be sure to represent the sounds accurately. In human speech, most consonants are short and usually don't take up more than 1 or 2 frames. Vowels, however, can be any length. If a person is shouting, for instance, you may have vowels topping 30 frames in length. In these cases, it is important that you don't simply hold the mouth in the exact same position for more than a second—it would look unnatural. Instead, create two slightly different mouth positions and keep the mouth moving between them so that the character looks alive.

Exercise #2: Reading a Track

Let's take a line of dialogue and read it for animation.

1. On the CD-ROM, choose the audio file called DIALOGUE.WAV if you use a PC, or choose DIA-LOGUE if you use a Mac. Load the appropriate file into your favorite sound editing program. The dialogue says, "Oh no, they're on to me." At 30fps, the dialogue measures about 120 frames.

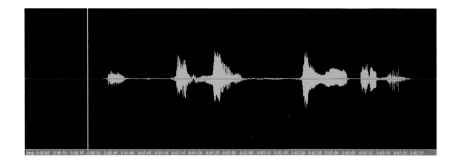

After you the load the file into your sound editor, this dialogue file looks something like the image to the left.

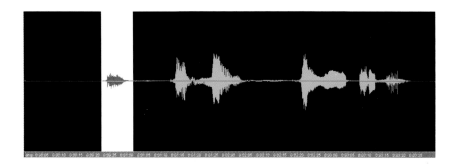

The first sound in the file is a gasp that runs from frames 22 through 30.

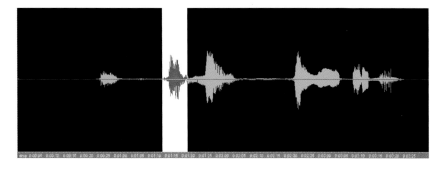

continues

Exercise: continued

The next big hunk of sound is the word "Oh," which runs from frames 42 through 49.

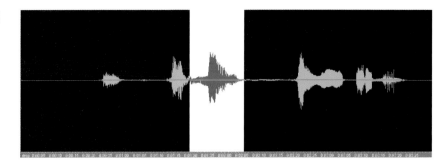

After that is the word "No."

2. Work through the entire track, writing down the positions of each phoneme. The following is a graphic representation of where the phonemes fall.

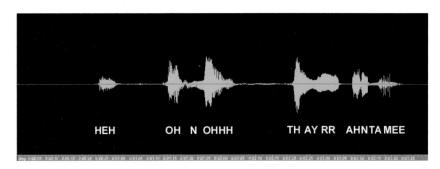

Animating Dialogue

Now that you've read the track, you're ready to begin animating the dialogue. Dialogue is slightly different from lip sync, because lip sync simply involves the lips. Dialogue, however, involves the whole character. When animating characters, be sure to get the character's entire body into the acting.

Mouth or Body First?

With the body so important to dialogue, one of the questions you might have is whether to animate the mouth or the body first. In cel animation, animators are forced to draw the mouths last, because it makes no sense to draw mouths on a character until the animation of the body is drawn. In stop motion, the mouths are done at the same time as the body. In CG, it's really not that big an issue, because any part of the animation can be tweaked independently of the others.

Some animators simply do the mouth first just to get the tedious task out of the way. It also is easier to get the mouth animated first on a still head rather than on one that is moving. Another good reason to do the facial first is to get the rhythm of the track. At a certain point, you no longer hear the words and instead hear the "beats" in the track. This enables you to animate the body much better, because you know where the major accents are in the track.

Other animators like to concentrate on the body first and then get the mouths. Many times this is done for characters who have extremely broad gestures—characters who "talk with their hands." Both approaches work equally as well, and because you can always go back and tweak the body and the lips independently, the line between the two methods is pretty much a grey area. For this particular animation, let's start with the lips and then move on to the eyes, head, and body.

Animating the Mouth

If the track is read properly, the phonemes and their location are pretty much known. In the track you just read, for example, you know there is a gasp at frame 22 and the word "Oh" at frame 42. One important trick that works to your benefit is to always try to open the mouth quickly and close it slowly.

Vowels

Vowels are those points in speech where the mouth opens. When animating a vowel, you need two positions. The first position is the accent pose, when the vowel is first uttered. The second position is the cushion pose, which happens toward the middle-to-end of the vowel sound. The accent usually has the mouth open wider than the cushion. One good way to do this is to animate the jaw so it closes slightly as the vowel progresses. For fast vowels of only 2 frames, this may not be much of an issue, but this rule of thumb applies to anything above 4 frames.

In the dialogue track you read, for example, the first word "Oh" takes approximately 7 frames to complete. In this time period, the mouth needs to travel from wide open (accent) to the lips closed and pursed into an oooh sound (cushion). At frame 42, you open the jaw and then animate its value lower through frame 49 as the jaw closes. Simultaneously, you add the oooh pose, which rises in value from somewhere around frame 42 through 49.

On the CD

For reference, on the CD, there is an animation of just the mouths for the dialogue read previously, called DIALMOUTH.AVI.

Consonants

Consonants are those points where the mouth closes. With the possible exception of a long M, F, or V sound, most consonants are only a few frames in length; some can be less than 1 frame long. With this in mind, make sure you leave each position on the screen long enough for the audience to read it. At 24 or 30 fps, consonants must be on the screen for at least 2 frames in order to be read. If the consonant is too short, steal time from a vowel or combine two consonants into one.

Eyes and Dialogue

After the basic lip sync is accomplished, the eyes are next on the list. When animating eyes with dialogue, be sure you understand where the character needs to be looking. Ask yourself the question, "Who is the character talking to?" Try to keep the eyes focused on the subject at hand.

Of course, there are places where a character may need to look away. People who are nervous tend to give darting glances. A dishonest person's eyes may be somewhat shifty. Don't be afraid to change the shape of the eyes and brows as the dialogue requires. A character whose eyes remain the same shape throughout a line of dialogue appears lifeless.

On the CD

For reference, on the CD, there is an animation of the mouths and eyes called DIALEYES.AVI.

Blinks are also very important. They accompany most major head motions, so if the head turns or bobs to accent a phrase, you need to blink the eyes as well. Dead spots in the dialogue are also good places to sprinkle in a blink or two. Blinks can also be storytelling tools; shy or lying people tend to blink a lot, for example.

Head Motion and Dialogue

The head moves quite a bit when people talk. The head bobs, nods, and shakes to emphasize certain words in a line of dialogue. When speaking loud sounds, the head usually raises to help open the throat. This is helpful when animating the loud sounds or accents in speech.

When animating an accent where the head raises, it is always a good idea to anticipate the motion by lowering the head three or four frames before the accent and then popping up the head on the accented syllable. This is also known as a head bob, and can be accompanied by a blink. To get more action into the head bob, you can also get the body into the action. As the head moves down in anticipation of the accent, raise the shoulders a bit. As the head pops up, lower the shoulders. Taken to extreme, this type of motion is the same as used in the classic cartoon "take."

In the track you just read, a good place for a head bob might be as the character says, "Oh no." As he says "Oh," lower the head, popping it up at the start of the word "no." You can overshoot this pose a bit and then settle into a more relaxed pose by the end of the word "no."

Body Language and Dialogue

When talking, many people use their hands to clarify and emphasize the major points of their speech. Getting this part of the animation correct is a lesson in acting. If you want to see how not to animate, watch some really nervous or first-time actors. They usually are very self-conscious, stuffing their hands in their pockets, wringing them nervously, or hanging their hands loose at their sides.

In real life, body language precedes the dialogue by anywhere from a few frames to as many as 20. Generally, a slow, dim-witted character has more time between gestures and dialogue than a sharp, quick character. Speedy Gonzales has considerably less lead time on his gestures than Forrest Gump. Someone giving a long, boring speech is much slower than a fire-and-brimstone evangelist.

You should also make an effort to ensure that your gestures fit the dialogue smoothly. The first gesture every animator learns is the ubiquitous finger-point for emphasis, followed soon after by the fist pounding into the palm. These gestures certainly have their place, but within a much larger palette. Simply watching people in their natural habitat is always your best reference.

One of the better ways to animate the body for use with dialogue is with pose-to-pose animation. Listen to the track to the point where you understand the major "beats" of the track—where a character gives emphasis to a word, pauses, or otherwise changes cadence. Because the body moves a few frames ahead of the dialogue, place your major poses slightly ahead of these beats. When the poses sync up with the dialogue, allow the computer to in-between these poses, and then go back on a second pass to tweak.

Exercise #3: Animating the Dialogue

Now that you've gotten some advice as to how to proceed, animate your character speaking the dialogue you track-read. Assign the mouth shapes, and then get the eyes, head, and body moving in sync. Render a test, and then go back and fine-tune the animation until you are satisfied.

On the CD

On the CD, there is an animation of the mouths, eyes, and head motion called DIALHEAD.AVI.

On the CD

For reference, the final test on the CD is called DIALFINAL.AVI.

When animating dialogue, get the entire body into the act.

Conclusion

This chapter presented the fundamentals of dialogue animation. The fundamentals are easy to understand and grasp, but getting your animations to look good requires some more work. Now it is time for you to practice, practice, and practice some more. You should record some tracks of your own and animate some more characters. If you are shy in front of a microphone, there are many ways to get dialogue besides hiring a voice actor. One way is to find some dialogue worth using in an old movie. Pick a scene from your favorite movie and animate a character speaking the dialogue. Of course, if you want to distribute such a film commercially, you run into copyright problems and need to get all sorts of permissions. For practice use only, however, it's not an issue. Another way is to record a normal everyday conversation and animate that. Wherever you obtain your dialogue, remember to have fun when animating.

Suggested Readings

Suggested Readings

Anatomy Books

Anatomy Coloring Book
by Wynn Kapit, Lawrence M. Elson
ISBN: 0064550168

Great for learning all about the muscles, skeleton, and their connections. It's a hands-on exercise that helps you learn how the body moves and works. It also has every part of the body separated, so you don't see a shoulder area with *all* the muscles at once. Bottom line: Get this book and study it! You will become a better animator and create better skeletal setups.

Anatomy for the Artist
by Jeno Barcsay
ISBN: 07060716900

Amazing drawings of both the deep-layer muscle and superficial-layer muscles broken down with the skeleton. Lots of drawings that show how the skeleton moves underneath the skin in motion.

Melloni's Student Atlas of Human Anatomy
by June L. Melloni (Editor), Ida G. Dox,
H. Paul Melloni, Biagio John Melloni
ISBN: 1850707707

This book offers pages of each muscle, its origin of attachment, the insertion on the skeleton, and its action. You can easily use this book to set up complex relationships between your skeleton and your deformation tools to create the muscle movement that happens when joints flex.

Albinus on Anatomy: With 80 Original Albinus Plates
by Robert Beverly Hale, Terence Coyle
ISBN: 048625836X

Great reference, plus just a beautiful book of illustrated plates. Orders the muscles into three layers. Each section starts with a skeleton, and then a first, second, and third order of muscles.

Color Atlas of Anatomy: A Photographic Study of the Human Body
by Johannes W. Rohen, Chihiro Yokochi, Elke Lutjen-Drecoll
ISBN: 0683304925

If you need a reference for realistic textures of skin, bones, and insides...look no further. There are many color photos of cadavers and body parts. We bought it mostly for the texture information, but there is also plenty of other good information in this one.

Facial Expression
by Gary Faigin
Watson-Guptill ISBN 0823012685

This book delves deeply into the structure and musculature of the face as it applies to creating facial expressions. This book is a must for those wanting to create realistic facial animation.

Animation Books

The Illusion of Life - Disney Animation
by Fank Thomas and Ollie Johnston
Hyperion ISBN: 078686070

Written by the ultimate Disney insiders—two of the original "Nine Old Men"—this bible of animation has become a classic. It explains Disney animation from the ground up and is very complete. There are original sketches, flipbooks and explainations of how memorable movie sequences were made. Though it's a book written by pencil animators, the techniques described are those used by every animator—including those who animate with pixels.

Cartoon Animation
by Preston Blair
Walter Foster ISBN: 1560100842

Cartoon Animation is without a doubt one of the time honored classics of animation. This is a reprint that has been expanded and repackaged into a smaller format book that can actually fit on your bookshelf. For years, this was the ONLY book on animation, and Preston Blair is one of the masters, having animated for both Tex Avery and Disney during the golden age.

The Animator's Workbook
by Tony White
Watson Guptill ISBN 0823002292

An award-winning animator offers a complete course on the principles and techniques of drawn animation, covering every aspect of the process. The book covers all of the basics of animation, from dialogue to walking to squash & stretch and much more. This book has become a classic and it is a great book for any animator, regardless of medium.

Creating 3D Animation - The Aardman Book of Filmmaking
by Peter Lord & Brian Sibley
Harry N Abrams ISBN 0810919966

This book explains how to do real world 3D animation using clay and puppets. It was written by the people at Aardman, who have done some of the best clay animation ever. While it is grounded in stop motion techniques, many of these can be translated to computer animation.

Timing For Animation
by Harol Whitaker and John Halas
Focal Press   ISBN: 024051310X

An excellent book that covers the subject of timing. The book deals with timing of characters as well as inanimate objects and effects such as fire.

Computer Facial Animation
by Frederic Parke, Keith Waters
AK Peters ISBN 1568810148

This book, while very technical, was written by one of the pioneers of facial animation. It has a number of techniques that still apply today.

Index

Numbers & Symbols